SEMI-DETACHED SUBURBAN MR JONES

Lewis Brian Hopkin-Jones (1942–1969).

A Rolling Stone from Cheltenham to Cotchford Farm

SEMI-DETACHED SUBURBAN MR JONES

Kevin J. Last

UNICORN

Published in 2024 by
Unicorn, an imprint of Unicorn Publishing Group
Charleston Studio
Meadow Business Centre
Lewes BN8 5RW
www.unicornpublishing.org

Text copyright © 2024 Kevin J. Last

All rights reserved. No part of the contents of this book may be reproduced, stored
in or introduced into a retrieval system, or transmitted, in any form or by any means
(electronic, mechanical, photocopying, recording or otherwise), without the prior
written permission of the copyright holder and the above publisher of this book.

Every effort has been made to trace copyright holders and to obtain their permission
for the use of copyrighted material. The publisher apologises for any errors or
omissions and would be grateful to be notified of any corrections that should be
incorporated in future reprints or editions of this book.

ISBN 978 1 916846 34 0
10 9 8 7 6 5 4 3 2 1

Design by newtonworks.uk
Printed in Malta by Gutenberg Press

Picture credits
in order of appearance:

Frontispiece: Associated Press / Alamy Stock Photo

Plate section
Plate 1: Kevin J. Last
Plate 2: PA Images / Alamy Stock Photo
Plate 3: Trinity Mirror / Mirrorpix / Alamy Stock Photo
Plate 4: Trinity Mirror / Mirrorpix / Alamy Stock Photo
Plate 5: Neville Marriner / ANL / Shutterstock
Plate 6: Alamy Stock Photo
Plate 7: Trinity Mirror / Mirrorpix / Alamy Stock Photo
Plate 8: Timo Tijhof / Wikimedia Commons
Plate 9: Kevin J. Last

CONTENTS

INTRODUCTION	1
THE MAIN PLAYERS AND PLACES	9
ISLAND IN THE STREAM	11
SPOTLIGHT: SLIDE GUITAR	28
THE TIES THAT BIND	29
SPOTLIGHT: THE ILLEGITIMATE CAST-OFFS	40
THE STONE AGE	41
SPOTLIGHT: JOHN (PAUL ANDREW) MOLLOY	60
YOU'D BETTER MOVE ON	62
SPOTLIGHT: MOROCCO	70
COTCHFORD FARM – THE DARK SIDE	72
SPOTLIGHT: ANITA PALLENBERG	100
WHEN BLUE TURNS TO GREY	102
SPOTLIGHT: ALEXIS KO[E]RNER	109
THIS COULD BE THE LAST TIME	111
SPOTLIGHT: HARTFIELD, EAST SUSSEX	133
RELATIONSHIPS	134
SPOTLIGHT: DR C. M. MILROY'S REPORT	140
GET OFF OF MY CLOUD	141
SPOTLIGHT: GEORGE HARRISON	147
AFTERMATH	149
BACKGROUND	160
ACKNOWLEDGEMENTS	163
BIBLIOGRAPHY	164
INDEX	165

This place is me, man ... I'll never leave here I'm sure.

Brian Jones, on arriving at Cotchford Farm.

INTRODUCTION

This is my third and final book based round three residents of Cotchford Farm in Hartfield, East Sussex. In the first I told the story of William Young, a gentleman farmer's son who left the farm in 1853 to work in the mills surrounding Lake Erie in Canada. He left behind a diary which is a window on the world of the mid-19th century. In the second I turned my attention to Christopher Robin, who spent much of the 20th century trying to escape from the effects of his father's highly successful creation, Winnie-the-Pooh. In these stories, Cotchford Farm acts a dumb witness to two very different situations. In both accounts I examined the lives of two sons with a close affiliation to Cotchford Farm, where it represented both a working farm and a family home. In the second case, it formed the catalyst for the magic kingdom of Hundred Acre Wood. While the first two tell stories of how the property was used in relation to the circumstances that prevailed at the time, the third and final volume operates like a corruption of historical Cotchford and everything it previously stood for. Fortunately it only lasted a few months, yet it remains a nasty scab in its history that, despite the near 60 years that have elapsed since, it refuses to completely go away, largely because the investigation at the time seemed unsatisfactory.

In this account Cotchford becomes the setting for something of a horror story and eventually a tragedy played out in the finest surroundings to someone who, with his short stature and blond mop of hair, appeared as if, at least to his housekeeper, to be a modern-day Winnie-the-Pooh. Given Brian Jones' wild history, this seems extraordinary. The two could not have been less alike.

The story carries two major themes; a self-inflicted, almost total waste of young life and talent and an extraordinary cruelty forced on him and others by an old school East End villain. Amazingly, what happened appears to have never been thoroughly investigated and yet it carries with it that same sense of eventual separation from Cotchford Farm that underlines the previous stories, but in a very different and much more dramatic way. When a well-known person comes to grief in the way that Brian Jones did, you would think that would trigger a very careful set of enquiries. However, it seems strange to report that, often with celebrities and especially in this case, where a Rolling Stone was the victim, the opposite seems to be true. Perhaps the only thing that all three of my residents shared was an initial love of Cotchford, its surrounding East Sussex countryside and, of course, the Hundred Acre Wood in which A. A. Milne weaved his literary magic.

I was born just five years after Brian Jones so I feel as if he was something of a contemporary and although I never had any of his musical skills, I did have a fascination with The Rolling Stones and remember wondering how their life could be so very different to mine, growing up north-west of London and on the very edge of suburbia. My life was proscribed and controlled while theirs seemed to be the very opposite, wild and unregulated in a way that was entirely new to the postwar generation and even more so to their parents who must have wondered what they had fought a war for if this was to be the result. So, not unnaturally, there was a strong edge of disapproval in the parents while the generation below them viewed the change with something more like curiosity. Where the parents thought it was disrespectful to everything they had been through (perhaps with good reason), their offspring regarded it as a possible gateway into a completely new world. While we are talking here about popular culture, it was not in any way limited to music but revealed itself in the other arts in various ways and particularly in film, where directors had decided to push against the boundaries of censorship; anything from nudity to extreme violence.

An early example of straining against the borders of what was acceptable came in the form of Alfred Hitchcock's *Psycho* (1960), which, in its curiously destructive way, has never been bettered as a horror film and which was directed by a man who was about 60 at the time. So it was not simply the young who wanted to push the boundaries of good taste to the limit and sod the consequences. In some ways it is possible that we are still on that road to make the unacceptable acceptable, to make language that would have been originally thrown out in films and television in earlier years more of the common denominator, so that now you have to look really hard

Introduction

to find something to watch on television that would not make Grandma blush until, of course, you find out that she too is not beyond that language in the way you thought she would be. As to whether we are any better off for allowing our guard to slip is contentious, given that crimes against the person are being committed in ways that once we would never have dreamed of and violence, in the shape of multiple shootings and stabbings, is taking place all over the planet, largely unchecked by successive weak governments who seem to let these matters pass them by. When a girl student can stab her teacher, as recently happened in Wales, we must surely be on a downward path.

What were previously largely safe places resonant of 1950s England have now become those where you have to watch where you go and when, if you want to remain in one piece. There are still occasional media forays into the past as in the recent *The Marlow Murder Club* (2024) which suggests an older, safer environment until you realize that is just a modern version of *Midsomer Murders* that celebrates the countryside rather than the dodgy people who live in it. Not that I am suggesting that The Rolling Stones were responsible for all that went wrong in the early 1960s, but certainly Brian Jones was a textbook example of what can happen if you set out on an unchecked and hedonistic lifestyle, as he himself eventually recognized. We might have imagined for the rest of the band that it was largely a pose, a stage act, even though there was an element of drug taking. LSD was a new experience then. Unfortunately that spilled over into real life with lurid headlines about Marianne Faithful, and even found a niche in the 1970 film *Performance* directed by Nicholas Roeg where Mick Jagger could be found, resplendent with rouge lips, in bed with groupie Anita Pallenberg and another. This gangster-style epic appalled the distributors, Warner Bros, with its decadent scenes of drug taking and violence. It also demonstrated the lengths members of The Rolling Stones went to in their efforts to gain attention and shock and how, for Brian Jones, this fiction metamorphosed into fact for the period at the end of his short life. Looking back, it may have been about a search for ultimate pleasure after the restrictions of wartime, but there was often no pot of gold at the end of this deceptive rainbow and the generation throwing themselves into it were not the ones who fought

Semi-Detached Suburban Mr Jones

and died for their country. It was a reaction without anything obviously experienced to react to, and to the parents, it seemed like a betrayal of all the young people who lost their lives fighting against Hitler, the madman who seems to have been regenerated today in the more dangerous Putin.

This is an altogether darker tale, one where the subject becomes caught up in a dangerous spiral of drink and drugs, the bleak underside of fame. And yet, just like Jones' predecessor, it starts and ends with a relatively privileged middle-class boy who thought that Cotchford would be both the country retreat that proved he had 'made it' and a place to chill out, away from the pressures of being a member of The Rolling Stones. He also was greatly enchanted with its connection to Winnie-the-Pooh and its romantic associations. He used to regularly read from it. But there was another reason. It was a comfortable distance from London and the attentions of police sergeant Norman Pilcher, a man who had continually harassed Jones and other pop stars who had pushed the limits with their indulgence in drugs. Pilcher also undoubtedly had an axe to grind and Jones was an easy target.

Yet, in all other respects the story could not have been more different from the Milnes', having more in common with the Michael Barrymore case or even Profumo and its setting round a swimming pool than the enchanted world of Pooh. What is it about swimming pools, ostensibly places of fun and relaxation, that often turn sour? It must surely be the presence of water, elemental and occasionally dangerous. Due to the presence of undesirables, it proved to be exactly that in the case of the original Rolling Stone; a place of destruction. The history of Brian Jones, of The Rolling Stones, is a dark retelling of a latter-day Christopher Robin gone desperately and impossibly uncontrolled. It could be interpreted as a morality tale for the end of the hedonistic sixties, demonstrating how the unbridled desire for drugs, fame, money, music and women can bring you crashing down. Moving to Cotchford Farm for Brian Jones was not the relief it was intended to be, but rather became the setting for a small and intimate tragedy that seemed, in the aftermath, rather pathetic.

Jones may be a common name, but Brian was by no means a common man, singling himself out for special attention from an early age. To understand him properly, we need to go back to wartime Cheltenham where he lived his

Introduction

early years. It was also Cheltenham and, in particular, the town cemetery, which became the final resting place for this ultimate rock and roller, cancelled first by his father and then by the band that he himself had formed. We need to examine what happened in the years between his birth in 1942 and 1969, the year of his death. It is ironic that, in his spare time, his father regularly played the organ in St Mary's Parish Church but, as a person, seemed to totally lack any sense of warmth, love or Christianity that you might expect. His music can almost be seen as a prescient early tribute to his son but before the fact. Ultimately, the story is about Brian's inability to cope with life, his frightful judgement and his misuse of almost everything and everyone who came his way. This lack of stability meant that he was doomed before he started, set to follow a downward path that could only end in one way; destruction.

While it provides some necessary background, this volume is not intended to be a comprehensive history of the life of Brian Jones or The Rolling Stones, which have been well covered elsewhere. Rather, it concentrates on the circumstances that led him to make the fateful decision to buy Cotchford Farm in an effort to be seen not simply as a mindless rocker but as a future country gentleman, reverting, as it were, to his middle-class roots. However, Jones was far too conflicted and taken up with himself ever to make this work but even he could not possibly have envisaged the horrors to come. And, sadly, he was too weak a personality to do anything about them. The middle-class boy from conservative Cheltenham identified himself, almost from the off, as richly talented but deeply selfish, and very quickly allowed his life to run out of control. In so doing, he created innumerable problems for his parents and himself and upset the lives of many who came in contact with him. He was the archetypal example of a rock star who, instead of embracing his talent and maximizing it, set out on the short highway to ultimate destruction. The damage he did to others; his parents, his countless girlfriends and even himself, is quite remarkable in so short a span. That some of the girls he wronged loved him is without question, but Jones was set on a course where only one thing mattered – himself. He could never consider anyone else for more than a moment: he was a narcissist. Yet it gave him no satisfaction. He was like a searchlight that

Semi-Detached Suburban Mr Jones

temporarily illuminates everything close by, both people as well as things, and then is gone, never to return. What one is left with is a stream of wasted talent, lives and unfinished business. That he was a star there is no doubt but, like the brightest shooting stars, he soon fell to earth leaving behind a sea of grief. There is no doubt that one of the mantras of the entertainment industry is that if you want the world to remember you, die young. Brian Jones fulfilled that supremely well, just like Jimi Hendrix.

We often think of Mick Jagger as the leader of The Rolling Stones and it may have been the case now for many years but what has been largely forgotten, almost expunged from history, was that Brian Jones founded the group and, if it were not for him, Jagger, Richards and the others would never have got their opportunity. To start with they were initially far less experienced and much of what they learned, they learned from Brian. So, to Jones, forming and running a top band was his life. It is what he really wanted to do but unfortunately, he did not have sufficient strength of character or organizational ability to keep going what he had undoubtedly started.

All we have now, more than 50 years later, as the remaining members grow old and die off is a relatively anonymous headstone in Cheltenham Cemetery.

'In Affectionate Remembrance of Brian Jones.'

Brief and to the point, this epitaph shares the lack of emotion that typifies his father, Lewis. The dedication gives no clue to the nature of the man himself. It is this that I want to clarify because it could all have been so different. There have been a number of attempts to cover this story previously, some by those involved, but they have sometimes been written by those with an axe to grind either in anger or in grief. What is undoubtedly true is that most of these leave many questions unanswered and prove, if proof were needed, that Brian Jones' short life on this planet was nevertheless responsible for both disturbing and ruining a number of lives. From the very start he was a risk to others and eventually he became a risk to himself. Often disgraceful while showing flashes of genius, he was certain to crash and burn. Yet, even those who he had wronged sometimes forgave him and if they could not have him in life, fought for a piece of his legacy afterwards. In each case, they are just part of an incomplete story, just as Jones' life was incomplete and his death unsatisfactorily explained. It is a modern tragedy without proper closure, leaving a pall of uncertainty hanging over it. Death by mis-adventure may be a convenient explanation but it is a wholly inadequate label. Despite being an asthmatic, Jones was a strong swimmer and there were others who had good reason to wish him gone. But, and we should be clear on this, there is no suggestion that the other Stones themselves were in any way involved. They may have wanted him out of the band but there were good reasons for that, he was holding them back, and that's as far it goes. The true cause lies elsewhere and there is no doubt they were extremely shocked by his demise.

Swimming pools and the shower in *Psycho* (1959), while appearing to offer a pleasurable experience, carry a sense of threat. There are numerous examples but, as in the Barrymore case, it is the unspoken deeds around them that are left strangely unexamined. After more than 50 years, we can now look at the case of Brian Jones in a colder, more analytical light. The problem is that rereading the accounts of all those involved leaves a diffi-culty. There are just so many different versions of the same story, varying from witness statements that seemed to have been sanitized, to opinions passed many years later when the trail had gone cold. There is also a void at the centre. For this reason, I have attempted to contain this account to those involved who matter most in the narrative rather than include every bit player. It makes the whole thing easier to understand.

Predictably, after his death those who knew him came out with thoughtful eulogies praising his skills although, for the most part, they were signifi-cantly lacking before he died. Alexis Korner and George Harrison were the exceptions, probably because they were as close as anybody was to being soulmates. And, while it was much easier for those in the musical world to recognize his skills and praise him, they did not have to live with him on a day-to-day basis. There was the resentment that came, often unjustifiably, from his family as well as, quite justifiably, from the long list of people who he let down, namely the families of those (at least) five illegitimate children that he fathered and then quite callously abandoned. The mothers of these children may have been naïve in expecting anything else but it

Semi-Detached Suburban Mr Jones

must have been quite a burden to observe on the one hand his burgeoning success and the money that brought in, while they were often living close to the breadline or were dependent on their own parents to try and make good the shortfall. Yet, despite all this and rotten treatment, many of them continued to carry a candle for him. In addition to them, there are the variety of circus hangers-on who choose to keep him alive, like Jacqui Saunders who, according to Geoffrey Giuliano,

> ... claims she has regular contact with Jones via the spirit world.
> (197, 1994)

So, in the following chapters, I will try to piece together the various aspects of the life of Brian Jones and how what went before, although not specifically connected, culminated in a frightening final act.

N.B. Quotations are indented and show the page and publication date of the book concerned in brackets afterwards. Any spelling/grammar discrepancies therein have been left intact.

It is possible to read this book quickly by omitting the *Spotlight* sections since their purpose is merely to develop certain elements touched on in the narrative.

THE MAIN PLAYERS AND PLACES

Andrews, Patricia. Ex-Boots employee who found common ground with Jones in the Cheltenham coffee bars.

Appleby, John. Jones' great friend, substitute father figure and mentor early in his career.

Carter-Fea, Jim. Manager of the Revolution Club, London.

Cheltenham. A spa town in Gloucestershire. Important because it is central to the background of who Brian Jones was and the contrast to what he became.

Cotchford Farm. The 16th-century farmhouse that Jones bought in 1968 as a country retreat to get away from the rough and tumble of the London-based band and because of its association with Winnie-the-Pooh.

Dunbar, John. Marianne Faithful's husband.

Faithful, Marianne. Singer and one-time girlfriend of The Stones.

Fitzsimons, Joan (aka Jackie). Initially mistress to Frank Thorogood.

Gibbs, Christopher. A friend of Brian's.

Gore, Roger. Schoolfriend of Brian's.

Hallett, Mary. Housekeeper at Cotchford Farm and one of Brian's true supporters.

Hattrell, Dick. A family friend whose home offered a haven to the often disapproved-of Jones.

Jones, Barbara. Sister. b. 22nd August 1946.

Jones, Lewis Blount. Father and aeronautical engineer. (1917–2009)

Jones, Lewis Brian Hopkin. 28th February 1942–2nd July 1969. Founder of The Rolling Stones.

Jones, Louisa Beatrice (née Simmonds). Mother. (1918–2011)

Jones, Pamela. Sister. 3rd October 1943–14th October 1945 (died of leukaemia).

Keylock, Tom. Ex-army man who became The Stones' efficient but pugnacious and latterly, somewhat dubious road manager. (1926–2009)

Semi-Detached Suburban Mr Jones

Klein, Allen. American manager of The Rolling Stones after Andrew Oldham.

Korner, Alexis. Leader of the influential rhythm and blues band that Brian Jones was asked to join.

Lawrence, Linda. Girlfriend and mother to Brian's child, Julian.

Lawson, Janet. Girlfriend of Tom Keylock.

Marshall, DCI Robert. Lead detective in the investigation.

Oldham, Andrew Loog. The Rolling Stones' manager.

Pallenberg, Anita. German/Italian girlfriend to Brian Jones who lost her to Keith Richards.

Palastanga, Brian. Chauffeur to Brian Jones when with The Rolling Stones.

Pates Grammar School in Cheltenham. Where both the best and worst of Brian Jones began to come to the fore.

Pilcher, Norman. Police sergeant with a penchant for nailing pop singers taking drugs.

Potier, Suki. Model and Brian's girlfriend for a time at Cotchford Farm.

Stewart, Ian. Band member and eventually roadie before Keylock took over.

Taylor, Bernie. Pat Andrews' brother-in-law from whom Jones rented a flat after leaving home.

The Rolling Stones. Mick Jagger, Keith Richards, Bill Wyman and Charlie Watts.

Thorogood, Frank. East End hard man and so-called building contractor. Schoolfriend of Keylock.

Wohlin, Anna. Swedish dancer, final girlfriend of Jones, principally at Cotchford Farm.

Ziyadeh, Mushasier Yusef. Jordanian boyfriend of Joan Fitzsimons.

'I'm very glad I knew Brian Jones, the errant musical phenomenon I believe him to have been, and he was definitely a one-off the likes of whom I have not encountered again in my life.'
Roger Gore, schoolfriend. (2019)

ISLAND IN THE STREAM

Lewis Brian Hopkin-Jones was born on the 28th February 1942, the son of a Welsh aero engineer also called Lewis and his wife Louisa, in the Park Nursing Home in Cheltenham. The house they lived in at that time was called Rosemead, situated in Eldorado Road in the Lansdown area of that town. This was a pleasant substantial house befitting of his father's work and status, and it seems ironic that Eldorado suggests that golden place that Brian sought but never achieved.

Since it was 1942 when Brian was born, it is certain that Lewis's skills were in substantial demand towards the war effort. Brian's earliest years were spent in the fairly sheltered and buttoned up atmosphere of wartime Cheltenham suburbia extant at the time. Tragedy marked both the beginning and end of Brian's life in that he lost his baby sister, Pamela, to leukaemia when he was just three and, even at this early age, this was the start of his troubles. His parents, locked in grief, kept their pain to themselves and excluded Brian from their mourning. This was to set the pattern for the years ahead. According to Geoffrey Giuliano:

> Lost and alone, the little boy wandered round the hushed, strained house in terrified confusion, fearing his beloved sister had been given away and that he too might share the same fate. (3, 1994)

Since Giuliano wasn't there and probably had no way of knowing, this might have seemed like a flight of fancy except that Jones himself confirms it.

> I remember this awful feeling of doom and gloom. My poor sister. I had no idea what had happened to her. I was terribly afraid. Instead of drawing me closer my parents seemed to push me away. But why? What had I done to anyone? It still hurts terribly to this day. (3, 1994)

Outside things were somewhat easier, in that Brian was remembered by neighbours,

Semi-Detached Suburban Mr Jones

> … contentedly roaming the pavements with his pet goat, and his inseparable feline companion, Rollader. (3, 1994)

However, Giuliano does get the name of Jones' dead sister wrong, calling her Pauline when it should have been Pamela.

Brian was a sickly child suffering from croup, an inflammation of the larynx and trachea, otherwise known as the windpipe. It is associated with breathing difficulties which he was never able to throw off and became prone to chronic bronchitis and asthma which later influenced his performance as a musician and may have contributed to his demise. This undoubtedly prevented him at times from playing with other children, leaving him on the sidelines. It was only when he found music that he found a lifelong interest and this in turn gave him an entrée to other opportunities, his skill in picking up both instruments and tunes being remarkable. Geoffrey Giuliano says:

> Young Jones was no longer alone. He found in music his one true companion. (4, 1994)

Brian went to Dean Close Preparatory School of good reputation, also in the Lansdown area of Cheltenham, and it was there that the staff first recognized his musical ability and where he learned to play the clarinet. This is very apt since for pretty much the rest of his life, music formed the mainstay. He was given an acoustic guitar for his 17th birthday, which he treasured. But Brian was let down by his own weaknesses and, surprisingly for a middle-class boy, a total failure to understand how to behave. Despite his interim associations with both his fellow band members and his girlfriends, Brian's short life was relatively solitary in that, according to most contacts, he was quite hard to know. The general perception of his girlfriends was often that, in any relationship, both parties were in love with the same man. So, if he never gave much away, that would seem to have been a hangover from a lonely childhood and a sense of holding back. He did little for others and was prone from an early age to inappropriate and sometimes downright cruel practical jokes, as we shall see.

But, to start with, his parents were quite delighted that Brian had inherited their own keen appreciation of music. Louisa was a piano teacher and, in his spare time, Lewis was organist and choir director for St Mary's Parish

Church in Cheltenham. They were solid and sensible if unimaginative citizens. His parents hoped that Brian could become a classical pianist, given his remarkable ability to both quickly absorb musical theory and to sight read.

> Revelling in his parents' all too occasional display of approval he excelled at a rate which astonished his teachers. Before long, he picked up the recorder and clarinet with equal ease. (4, 1994)

Lewis had also, at one time, considered Brian might become a dentist but neither of these two accredited careers were ever realized, despite his remarkable musical ability and above average intelligence. Lewis wanted Brian to become a key player in an orchestra, something that would be an ongoing credit to a quite talented family. And let there be no doubt about it. Both Lewis and Brian were decidedly ambitious, the former in a quiet way. For Brian though, music was his new love and the loneliness he had experienced as a small child began to dissipate.

One of his schoolfriends at Pate's Grammar School, Roger Gore, is able to provide a good deal of information about the young Brian. He lived outside Cheltenham in the village of Winchcombe and was a contemporary at this honourable establishment with a history going back to 1574.

> We were born in February 1942 exactly three weeks apart, I being the older, and we spent the first year grouped alphabetically in separate forms. It wasn't till 1954 that we became classmates, when we were both placed, according to our test results, in the A stream which was selected to take 'O' levels a year earlier than the other forms. He was obviously academically promising … Brian and I didn't become good friends until probably the fifth form … when we were closely associated with another person, Barry Smith, in an increasing affinity regarding life as mid-teenagers; an interest in music and a decreasing willingness to abide by the stuffy old fashioned mores of the school. The three of us continued our friendship into the sixth form where Brian and Barry did two years at A level, which I also did … Brian and Barry took the harder discipline, Physics, Biology and Chemistry. (2019)

Semi-Detached Suburban Mr Jones

Regardless of his later attempts to kick over the traces, this account gives a previously unknown version of Brian working hard to achieve results, at least at the start of his time there. Gore also explains his early introduction to music:

> The three of us were keen music buffs and record collectors and together often visiting a record shop off the High St (named Maxwell's I think) in the lunch hour to talk music, sample records and purchase LPs. Musically our tastes were allied but with different nuances. Brian liked trad jazz at this stage … Brian became more and more blues orientated over time. (2019)

Gore goes on to confirm that:

> Brian, like me, was in no way sports orientated regardless of his asthma, whereas music was second nature to him. Both of us increasingly skived off sport as much as possible. (2019)

However, when he did partake of it, he was no slouch and often proved very able, just as he did at everything else.

Amusingly, Roger Gore tells us of an incident which was prescient of what was to come.

> There was an occasion when Brian was involved with a band in a community hall in Hatherley. I can't recall now whether he had organized it or was actually playing in it, but he had invited me … No sooner than we [Gore with a friend] had gone into the lobby of the hall than I was approached by a group led by [a] Teddy Boy in Edwardian garb obviously looking for trouble. We immediately beat a hasty retreat and ran off down the road with the yobs in pursuit and I only escaped by hopping onto the deck of a moving double decker that was just leaving its stop. (2019)

Another quite extraordinary incident occurred which reminds one of *Tom Brown's Schooldays*. Roger Gore takes up the story.

> There is one infamous incident that stands out very vividly in my mind that was known to the school authorities as the 'Protherough Affair' which finally damned Brian in the eyes of the Head Master

Island In The Stream

… I cannot recall if there was any specific reason for the antithesis between Brian and a final-year prefect named David Protherough, but Protherough exercised his official position as a prefect to excess and was generally a rather unpleasant abrasive individual … The prefect system in CGS selected those who would embrace authority and exercise discipline by proxy and they could set lines or even detention. By and large they were fascistic and generally disliked by the majority of students, but obviously preferred to teachers. Brian and Barry were the two people who elected to do something about the dictatorial Protherough and a third boy named Edwards was willing to engage in a fist fight with Protherough in an organised contest in the gym, reminiscent of a public school duel as if Protherough was a latter-day version of Flashman of Rugby School. Edwards also came from Winchcombe and was in the final year six form and didn't normally associate with us. He was a genuinely quiet unassuming person and I genuinely think he undertook the task in a spirit of righting a perceived wrong and cutting Protherough down to size. It has been said that the argument between Brian and Protherough was over a girl but I don't subscribe to that and I don't believe Edwards would have had any incentive to have fought Protherough by proxy on that basis. Brian wanted me to join him and Barry in the gym for the showdown at the appointed time in the lunch break but I declined as I could see the likely serious fallout and having elected to stay on in the third year sixth, whereas Brian and Barry had decided to leave. I agreed to meet the following Saturday in the town bus station. To my eternal regret I never kept the appointment, for whatever reason, and I feel a little guilty to this day every time I recall it. (2019)

And, after all that lead up, we are not even told who won or how the authorities reacted! The quaint village of Winchcombe is quite a way from Cheltenham so Brian and Roger's friendship was mostly contained within schooldays and the occasional outing.

When Brian started playing, strangely Roger Gore never saw him play professionally on this occasion nor indeed on any other, despite the best intentions.

I lived in Oxfordshire in 1964 when the Stones played in Aylesbury in Buckinghamshire and my wife and I had tickets. We battled through thick January fog to the Granada and saw the band but, ironically, Brian had not made it. (2019)

The reason why is explained in Bill Wyman's book, *Stone Alone: The Story of a Rock and Roll Band.*

I got on the Stones bandwagon bound for Aylesbury … Keith woke up long enough to observe 'here comes the fog' … our speed dropped to 15mph and we crept along. Our one hour trip had now taken three hours and we were on the outskirts of Aylesbury when Mick shouted as Brian's car loomed out of the fog and began to pass us heading in the opposite direction. We all yelled out of the windows, but were unheard and he disappeared into the fog. Brian never reappeared from that foggy sighting but we arrived in Aylesbury and played two concerts without him. (1990)

Roger Gore also makes the interesting observation that:

I wouldn't say Brian was 'well-liked', but he wasn't specifically disliked either. He was mentally very sharp and I've little doubt that had he been more conventional and compliant he would have done very well academically. Then the world would have lost what he did become and one of the most influential and significant bands of all time would not have come into being. (2019)

This tends to work against the extremes expressed in Giuliano's book. Gore goes on to explain that:

Brian had serious rebellious tendencies, and they certainly became more common from the fifth form, and increasingly so through the sixth form. The school uniform of grey flannel trousers, black blazer, polished black shoes and mortar board were an increasing anathema to the three of us. In reality the mortar board summed up the ridiculous public school like attitude of CGS [Cheltenham Grammar School] which was housed in a suitably Dickensian Victorian edifice [since moved]. In a mark of defiance, and simple sartorial awareness, the three of us wore suede shoes instead of polished ones

Island In The Stream

and trousers bought at a drapers across the road from the school …
I can't remember any of us smoking in school but, instigated by
Brian, the three of us certainly went into the snug of a small pub
off Winchcombe Street for a beer on a few occasions in lunch hour,
and such activity would have had serious consequences had it been
observed, especially as we were under age. (2019)

Despite starting off at CGS and working hard, the destructive element that came to characterize his whole life started coming into play. Roger Gore tells us that:

Brian, however, could take things much too far and, on one occasion,
I remember being in the Physics Lecture Theatre which had the
sloping floor accessible through a trap door. In those days a crate
of milk in one third pint glass bottles was provided daily and Brian
inexplicably took it into his head to throw his empty bottle down the
void to smash it, followed by several others. He was found out for
this by Conway the physics master … The incident is quite vivid in
my memory as it rather made me aware that Brian courted the sort of
trouble I didn't have the stomach for. (2019)

Giuliano describes how his talent extended way beyond music and his,

… genius IQ of 135. Easily mastering all academic disciplines, it
was the arts where he really excelled … Brian would pen imaginative
science fiction tales … In art class he transformed his love of trains
into spectacular locomotive designs of minute detail and accuracy.
(4, 1994)

Nick Broomfield, in preparing for his documentary, *The Stones and Brian Jones* (2023), recounts a conversation when he met Brian by accident on a train.

Then the big surprise was that he was really into trains and
trainspotting, which was not something I'd expected. He and Stu
[Rolling Stones road manager Ian Stewart] would go and buy bits for
their train sets when they were on tour, or go trainspotting together.
(42, 2023)

Semi-Detached Suburban Mr Jones

Given the extreme behaviour of The Stones at the time, this seems a curiously mundane contrast. More conventionally, he played clarinet in the school orchestra. His skill at English and art was remarkable but it was not long before Brian started showing signs of the lifelong rebellion that kicked into play and caused a continuing catalogue of disasters ending in his tragic death at Cotchford Farm. Surpassing all the foregoing ability was Brian Jones' amazing capacity to self-destruct. The super intelligent and hyperactive Jones began his long decline almost as soon as he achieved the age of reason and the sense of waste borne of the fact that he could not control himself gradually increased. As it did so, his parents became increasingly distant. So the story that unfolds is of almost unmitigated problems, unused skills, and untold harm to himself and others. It is punctuated by narcissism, women, drink and drugs. There was an overwhelming selfishness and it was mostly the women with whom be became involved who became his unfortunate victims. After that, the blonde-haired golden goose became only good for the pot.

It is often the case that those who show remarkable skills, enough sometimes to run countries, often carry with them equally negative facets that seem to be there for balance but sometimes tell against them. In Brian's case, that balance did not exist and it would be true to say that he never really got started as the dark side of his character always seemed to get the upper hand. Had he been able to rise above this and put his undoubted ability to good use, the story could have been very different. Reflecting how much his eventual destruction was down to him and how much to others is partly the purpose of this book.

Just how extreme and off the wall he could be became evident at an early age. A rebellious streak came to the fore in the hyperactive Jones which involved, according to Giuliano, dyeing the family pets with a range of food colourings, hiding his school uniform and spectacles and melting down his regiment of soldiers into a molten mass of hot lead. So for every talent, there seemed to be a counter and ineffably stronger need to destroy. Yet the latter appeared to become uppermost. Because he was so clever, he was effectively held back by the others in his class at school and this waiting time (while they caught up) bored him and encouraged him to misbehave.

Island In The Stream

Even had his parents made special arrangements to harness his talent, it is hard to believe that he would ever have kept to the straight and narrow. He wanted to push to the limits on everything that he attempted, to see what it would be like if things went spectacularly wrong. Transferring this to the real world, although he was incredibly inventive, there was this decidedly unpleasant desire to encourage disaster, to know what it would be like to see a plane crash or a mass pile-up on the roads. It was almost as if he did not want things to go well, to behave normally. So he was very different to his parents who were both highly disciplined, organized, controlled and dully respectable. Brian Jones was not remotely respectable. In sharp contrast to his background, he spent his short life fulfilling his desires no matter what the cost to other people, turning his back on the result and then denying responsibility. This, remarkably, even included theft.

Nevertheless, despite a range of minor infringements such as tramping through Pate's Grammar School in his football boots and persuading his classmates to forsake the daily milk break for beer, the headmaster was remarkably sanguine about Jones, balancing his indiscretions with his undoubted ability. Much of this appears to have been caused by frustration, that he was being held back by others of lesser ability. Despite Roger Gore's comments, he was encouraged to take up sport and despite his health issues:

> Brian excelled in a wide range of physical disciplines, from soccer
> to judo, and proved himself a swimmer and diver of outstanding
> stamina. (5, 1994)

We should keep the latter skills in mind when we come to consider how he met his end because they have a relevance to the narrative.

Sport to Jones was nevertheless mostly a waste of time and whenever he could, not just because of his asthma, he made excuses to get out of it. He found it, like so much else, largely boring and pointless. So, from the above, we can now picture a supremely talented young man who could take on virtually any subject at school and do well at it. When it came to exams, he didn't even need to revise to any extent. He was supremely capable at almost anything. Set this against what happened to him and our reaction can only be one of the most appalling waste of a life, of innate talent, which could have been put to so much better use.

Semi-Detached Suburban Mr Jones

As he grew up Jones soon began to feel very constricted by Cheltenham, a town that, despite his early years being in wartime, seemed to have largely escaped many of the problems of both world wars. Cheltenham stands by the River Chelt which rises at Dowdeswell and makes its way through the town to the River Severn. According to Wikipedia, it was recorded as a royal manor in the Domesday Book (as Chintenham), first noted in 803, and gained a Royal Charter in 1226. Following the discovery of mineral springs there in 1716, Cheltenham came under the steely gaze of Captain Henry Skillicorne (1678–1863) who saw an opportunity to promote the town as a holiday resort where people could take advantage of the healing properties of the springs. As co-owner of the property which contained the spring, he saw an opportunity for development. This came about through his 1732 marriage to Elizabeth Mason, also perhaps opportunistic, whose father had ignored the potential on his doorstep. Skillicorne built a pump to regulate the flow of water and erected an elaborate well-house complete with a ball-room and upstairs billiard room to entertain his customers. And this was just the start. Cheltenham's ideal position in the countryside made it ripe to be developed into the spa town that we know today. According to Giuliano, Keith Richards view was that:

> It is a very genteel city of old ladies where it used to be fashionable to take baths once a year at Cheltenham Spa. Now it's a seedy sort of place full of aspirations to be an aristocratic town. (5, 1994)

Driving through it in 2024, it seemed fairly gracious with more than its fair share of grand buildings, yet I detected a feeling of incompleteness, a lack of unity that seems hard to explain.

The town's aspirations have somehow failed to be fully realized despite its situation on the edge of the Cotswolds. As Richards goes on to say:

> Pretty in its own way, but Dullsville. It rubs off on anyone who comes from there. (5, 1994)

And that is very much to the point. Although Brian soon came to reject its stuffy atmosphere, there was nevertheless an element ingrained in him, that despite everything that happened to him, was still pure Cheltenham. Far from an awkward adolescent, he developed a studied persona that appeared

Island In The Stream

polite and gracious, looked up to by his schoolfriends but largely rejected at home.

However, the attractive and attentive façade masked something much more dangerous; the inability to hold back. And so it was in 1958 that he brought about the pregnancy of Valerie, a girl from the girls' grammar school next to Pate's. Whereas his friends just thought about what they might achieve with the opposite sex, Jones went headlong into this disaster. He was totally unconcerned at the result and he completely lacked any sense of responsibility for the harm he had done. His previous reckless activities could not begin to match this, and Brian, already the black sheep at home, had to be severely dealt with. He was sent abroad to Germany in the vain hope that Valerie would have an abortion. But Valerie had the child and then offered the boy for adoption. We are not told if any money changed hands courtesy of Brian's parents but it seems likely. Lewis, bastion of all things great and good in Cheltenham, would have hated this. As a result, it created a distance between himself and Brian that was lifelong, despite Brian's frequent and ever more desperate attempts to put matters right.

While his parents had hoped to hush up the resulting scandal, they did not succeed. It actually sent shock waves through the entire community, even getting reported in the local papers. The good matrons of the town were outraged. This can't be happening in Cheltenham! So from being a likeable if somewhat eccentric rogue, the pregnancy gave him a different image. Jones morphed into an ostracized and potentially dangerous rebel. The problem for Jones' parents was that he could not be permanently disposed of like a piece of waste paper. It became clear that despite his innate brilliance, to their chagrin he was never going to make Oxford or Cambridge which is really where he could have exercised his considerable skills. Instead he had become *persona non grata* with just about everyone. He simply could not be trusted with anything or anyone. The self-destructive trait dominated and overcame any sense of doing the right thing and, once more, withdrawing into himself, Jones was now something of an outcast from Cheltenham society, not that he ever aspired to belong to it. It was, in truth, an appalling waste of talent and boys from Pate's with less than half his ability soon overtook him and went on to successful careers. Genius has its price and although it was never remotely realized, that is what he could have been.

> When I left school I felt completely at sea. Everyone regarded me as a lazy, good-for-nothing layabout, including my parents, and I suppose I was in a way. (8, 1994)

A change was called for. The only immediate solution seemed to be travel and in 1959, at the age of 17, he took the hint and, armed only with a Spanish guitar, he hitch-hiked his way across Scandinavia. His parents were happy to have him out of their hair and he regarded this period with great affection, as a happy interlude without anyone trying to restrict him. He found an opportunity to exercise his musical talents with like-minded hippies but he also took advantage of the talent offered to him in the form of Scandinavian women. It is more than possible that one or more of these became pregnant but whether because of the geographical distance or something else, it is not reported. Absolutely nothing had altered and any thoughts that he might grow up, get a job and start acting responsibly were very soon dashed.

Eventually, he was forced to come home. There was nothing left in the coffers and he had run out of the indulgence shown to him by his Scandinavian contacts. Surprisingly, on his return he found things had begun to change in his favour and the counterculture that he had experienced abroad had begun to infiltrate even sleepy old Cheltenham. It came in the form of the coffee bars that had already swept across less protected and self-regarding parts of the country. It was a curious time that affected me as well and I can clearly remember my first taste of it, initially innocent, in the genteel form of The Bluebird Café in Northwood, Middlesex, then another bastion of middle-class respectability in the north-west of London. There on a Saturday morning the boys and girls of a certain age assembled to discuss the latest news and parties, much to the apprehension of the owners. They would rather have swapped us for older and more acceptable patrons.

I can remember discussing the risks associated with going into the nearby Ruislip Woods at the time where a character, wonderfully known as Naked Norman, wearing only a mack that Lt Columbo would have rejected, would suddenly leap out and expose himself to the unwary, but he wasn't

Island In The Stream

dangerous or violent. A delightfully petite blonde, Kathy, responded to a question put to her by a local journalist on this subject asking whether she found this alarming, stating, quite categorically, that she would never go into the nearby woods alone. As a result, this left hanging in the air rather more questions than answers.

The Bluebird, with its genteel net curtains, adjoining the high street, was no beatnik dive and only had daytime opening hours but it was illustrative of what was to come and develop in the larger towns where, on a Saturday night, the youth of the day, both respectable and less so, assembled to take advantage of the juke box and the space provided in the more accommodating venues to jive the night away. Not that The Bluebird Café ever had a juke box. That would have been far too radical but it did begin to ferment the beginning of temptation to the youth of that time in a way that the immediate postwar period had made impossible. Just too many shortages and little in the way of leisure money. Unfortunately for Brian Jones, it offered another false green light and invited him into a world where he could make the best of his musical skills but also enter into countless other poor relationships with girls. He appeared to completely lack any depth of character.

UK television was in its infancy but the ever so prim and proper BBC of the time was able to offer an opportunity to hear the latest records on *Juke Box Jury* (1959–1967) fronted by the urbane, besuited and respectable David Jacobs, where half a song would be played, discussed by a panel of often curiously chosen judges, like the writer and broadcaster Nancy Spain and the more appropriate Pete Murray, and then voted on. So pop music was given a coat of establishment respectability, although the BBC must have already been wondering where it would lead. The initial opening to the world of performance pop music on television was offered by such programmes as the insipid *Six Five Special* (1957–1958) with Pete Murray and, later, *Ready Steady Go* (1963–1966), though the latter was markedly more successful. These shows accelerated the trend in that fairly sedate dancing was now permitted in the studio and the chart toppers of the day were invited to come and perform their hits. Eventually this led on to the long running and most successful programme of this kind, *Top of the Pops*

23

Semi-Detached Suburban Mr Jones

(1964–2006). Young men and girls were invited to the studio to rock gently to their chosen favourites but in the resulting enthusiasm, things started to go wrong at the BBC with the predatory nature of some of the presenters and performers. What went on behind the scenes and in the dressing rooms became a matter of concern, especially when the mostly anodyne disc jockeys of the day were joined by the extraordinarily talentless but dangerous Jimmy Savile, who strangely managed to impress both the management, and even politicians, while remaining uncouth, talentless and, worse still, a threat. But it should be stressed, he was not entirely alone and even now, there may be some elderly DJs, perhaps only very occasional offenders, thanking their lucky stars that they were not caught up in Operation Yewtree which, partly successfully, sought to put matters right. However, as with so many of these investigations, it was too little too late and an awful lot of damage had already been done. It was this musical opening up and perhaps the risks it offered that appealed to Brian Jones.

The programmes mentioned encouraged the adolescents to go out and purchase a copy of the best hits to play on their scratchy old gramophones at home. If you really liked the artist, you might buy the LPs. These repeated the hits, in stereo sound if you were lucky, but other than in exceptional cases like The Stones and The Beatles, often most of the other tracks were rubbish; just there to justify the price. When you got fed up with the LPs there was a second-hand market for them; in my case in South Harrow market. At best you might get back half the original thirty-two shillings and sixpence purchase price but demand soon fell off along with the price as the market became saturated. This was not in any way a class thing. It's just that the middle classes tended to have more money to spend on non-essentials like records. It was also a step up, apparently, from the more passive Hornby Dublo model railway although now some would disagree. At least they didn't offer any kind of risk. The parents would find the latter an innocent and largely peaceful activity whereas pop music was something else for them to put up with after rationing and other wartime restrictions. It was also the beginnings of a temptation to misbehave and Brian Jones took full advantage of it. In the 21st century, model railways have made a strong comeback, often involving baby boomers who are trying to recapture their

Island In The Stream

lost youth, especially when the real thing is such an abject failure. One cannot but admire the strength of detail in the settings. So here we have the curious anomaly of Brian Jones being both innocently attracted to trams, trains and model railways while succumbing, at the same time, to the temptations and the fleshpots of the wider world.

This was the beginning of a new period of freedom for young people that simply hadn't been possible in earlier years. With the passing of the years, we may look on colourful San Francisco and Woodstock, NY (1969) with affection as enlightened abandonment of all the rules, a kicking away of all previous social structures. But it wasn't all good. The unlicensed sex had its consequences just as it did for Brian Jones and so did the drugs. The hippies may have looked colourful and spaced out but for those who had to live with them, they were not totally harmless, simply legless. Just because there was more leisure money in their pockets, it certainly was not being used to make them responsible citizens. Back in Cheltenham, Giuliano tells us that the opening of,

> … these often seedy hangouts with names like the Patio, Aztec and El Flamenco, attracted a wide spectrum of avant-garde artists, musicians and social outcasts, providing just the stimulation Jones's eager, restless mind craved. (8, 1994)

The names given to these music outlets often suggested the exotic but they were anything but, and those who frequented them were a mixture of the good, the bad and those unable to find respectable employment elsewhere. Brian honed his not inconsiderable musical skills in jazz combos wherever he could, his musical flexibility enabling him to switch groups whenever it was required. Observed at a distance by his disapproving parents, this was a long way from the classical musician they had in mind. It also, for them, was a waste of talent on a form of music that just didn't cut the mustard in traditional Cheltenham. It put him on the wrong side of the tracks. Something much more respectable was called for. And while this might strike as at last making use of Brian's musical talents and giving him something useful to do, the girls who inevitably frequented these dives became a target for the irresponsible Jones who seemed to have learned absolutely nothing from his own recent history.

This time it was not an underage girl who fell pregnant by Brian but a 23-year-old married woman from Guildford, at a so-called celebration of his 18th birthday. This was the second of Brian Jones' couplings which resulted in the birth of a baby, and these are just the ones we can be sure of. Once again the baby went full term but the resulting birth of a girl was never advised to Brian and, once again, he seemed to get away with his recklessness. As far as we can tell, he made absolutely no attempt to follow up on this indiscretion or indeed any other. It was all about him and everyone else was secondary. Creating new life and a family had absolutely no importance to him. As such it was a dark reflection of his own family's failure to include him as one of their own. It was 1960. According to Giuliano:

> In 1986 Stones' bassist Bill Wyman met up with the young woman and made a curious discovery. She'd uncovered her famous father's identity at age fifteen and upon investigation found in him similar behaviour patterns attributed to her bouts with epilepsy.
>
> 'I learned that sometimes he didn't know whether he was here, there, or anywhere. That tallied exactly with one of the epileptic symptoms I suffer from. I have since discovered there were so many times when Brian went ill. It's possible the epileptic symptoms I have are inherited from him.' (8/9, 1994)

So this got Wyman considering whether his extreme behaviour both in his relationships and as a member of the group could be an indicator as to what happened to him. Were his tantrums and his general wrong-headedness, his debility, caused by epilepsy? We will probably never know but this may help explain his outlook and why he often caused those with whom he came into contact so much grief. There is no doubt that, in addition to affecting himself and his contacts, this curious behaviour gave others, the more unscrupulous, a golden opportunity to take advantage of him and exploit his weakness for their own purposes. Many who associated with Jones found that his fecklessness meant that they had to wash their hands of him. He was just too unreliable. While this is understandable, we have to consider that his behaviour was as much or perhaps more down to illness as character. So the decision to condemn him outright should be reserved even if the desperate effect he often had on others remains the same. Easy to say, I know,

Island In The Stream

but, given his background, there must have been reasons why he was such a loose cannon.

Brian was both a musical genius and, in academic terms, he could turn his able mind to almost any subject successfully. Had he been able to set his mind on a career, steadily using these undoubted skills to better himself, he could have had a brilliant working life. Set against this was a voracious sexual appetite that knew no boundaries and was indulged without any concern for the consequences. This was also the sign of a very weak character and it was this latter aspect that eventually contributed to his downfall. There are many strong, talented people who suffer from an element of negativity, but it does not necessarily dull their effectiveness. The downside of Jones, plus the desire for drink and drugs, was unfortunately far stronger than the up. It was just supremely unfortunate that, in the most unlikely setting, this eventually placed him directly at the mercy of someone whose cold-hearted ruthlessness directly or indirectly led to his death.

SPOTLIGHT:
SLIDE GUITAR

According to Wikipedia, slide guitar is a technique for playing the guitar that is often used in blues music and therefore particularly appropriate to Brian Jones. It was originally of African origin. It involves playing a guitar while holding a hard object (a slide) against the strings, creating the opportunity for *glissando* effects and deep *vibratos* that reflect characteristics of the human singing voice. It typically involves playing the guitar in the traditional position (flat against the body) with the use of a slide fitted on one of the guitarist's fingers. The slide may be a metal or glass tube, such as the neck of a bottle, giving rise to the term 'bottleneck guitar' to describe this type of playing. It is more difficult to achieve than conventional playing and the strings are typically plucked (not strummed) while the slide is moved over the strings to change the pitch. The guitar may be placed on the player's lap and played with a hand-held bar (lap steel guitar).

Creating music with a slide of some type has been traced back to African stringed instruments and to the origin of the steel guitar in Hawaii. Near the beginning of the 20th century, blues musicians in the Mississippi Delta popularized the bottleneck slide guitar style, and the first recording of slide guitar was by Sylvester Weaver in 1923. Since the 1930s, performers including Robert Johnson, Robert Nighthawk, Earl Hooker, Elmore James (a hero of Brian's), and Muddy Waters popularized slide guitar in electric blues influencing later slide guitarists in rock music including The Rolling Stones, George Harrison (who was also interested in the sitar), Duane Allman and Ry Cooder. Lap slide guitar pioneers include Oscar 'Buddy' Woods, 'Black Ace' Turner, and Freddie Roulette. (2024)

THE TIES THAT BIND

Geoffrey Giuliano suggests that:

> Inevitably, the inquisitive mind and hyperactive temperament common in gifted children launched the emergence of a rebellious streak. (4, 1994)

Yet I would suggest, and I have known one or two gifted children, that rebelliousness is not inevitable. It is just that such children need to keep being specifically accommodated in recognition of their need to develop much more quickly than most. This puts a demand on both their parents and teachers, wondering just how far they can let their prodigy rise above their peers and what they need to do to achieve it. It also can create jealousy and ill feeling in those left behind. This was true of Lewis Brian Hopkin-Jones, the Welsh genius son unregulated by his staid parents, who started to infect others like a virulent and unstoppable disease and his parents wanted none of it. Instead of attending to his studies, he left behind him a trail of broken lives and broken dreams. When Brian developed a taste for jazz, it produced in his father a new horror which the stolid organist of St Mary's Church came to regard as the musical representation of depravity. It was for him the devil's own choice of music. Instead of maximizing himself, Brian went for the opposite.

Brian, as always frustrated, began what Giuliano calls,

> … a sequence of illicit trysts … leaving his stunned mates in gaping envy. (7, 1994)

However, this sense of approval is firmly denied by Terry Rawlings (2005) who, with Paul Spendel, describes exactly the opposite effect; that his peers thought he had gone too far.

> A school friend of his at the time commented, "The kids that had once been impressed by Brian now thought of him as a bad influence and just ignored him and left him out in the cold." (13, 2016)

Semi-Detached Suburban Mr Jones

I think this is much nearer the truth with Brian being regarded as an outcast, not just from his family, but from his peers. He was just too strange.

As we know, Lewis wanted Brian to progress to Oxbridge:

> I think the mild rebellion he displayed was due to the fact that at school they wanted him to be a scientist of some kind when essentially he was more inclined towards the arts. Had he devoted as much time to his studies as he did to music I think he would have been a brilliant scholar. Our clash was not so much one of personality as of ambition. (8, 1994)

This judgement on his son seems remarkably mild but we are not told to whom it was addressed or indeed at what point it was said. There is some doubt as to whether Lewis actually loved his son. There was little sign of it even though he had already lost one daughter. The problem that arose was due to a complete lack of common ground within the family and a failure by either party to find the right approach. So, unsurprisingly, Brian had to learn to become self-sufficient in that he kept his distance from the teenagers that frequented the Aztec and the other coffee bars. According to Giuliano (9, 1994), this was not too difficult because the traditional jazz musicians he was involved with were usually of a slightly older generation and, curiously, showed just the dedication in their line of country that Lewis had wanted for his son. The rejection by his parents and, more recently, his peers, was beginning to tell.

However, history began to repeat itself when he met sensible Patricia Andrews who, at the time, was just 15 and worked in Boots in Cheltenham. Yet Andrews had rather more about her than Brian's previous conquests. She felt sorry for the man who, despite being on the coffee bar circuit, seemed to spend much of his time on his own. As a result the determinedly working class but steely Andrews also felt she could better herself by learning from the cultured, well-spoken Jones. And so, surprisingly, another side of Brian Jones came to the fore, proving that he was not just a mindless, selfish yob. She was aware of his shady past but they found common ground in endless discussions on music. As a result she learned a great deal about the subject but also about Jones, whose sadness at the rejection by

The Ties That Bind

his family was palpable. It is also curious that, throughout his short life, there seems to have been very little input from his younger sister, Barbara. You might have thought that, with the early death of their older sister, they might have bonded, yet she scarcely figures in his life and certainly not in the usual close sense of siblings. What Andrews discovered in Brian was that music was his almost total concern: playing it, discussing it and experimenting with it.

Brian was fortunate in that he found a substitute father figure in John Appleby, a relationship he struck up at the El Flamenco club. According to Giuliano:

> Ten years older, with a kindly, unflappable manner, Appleby proved a steadying influence on the often confused, insecure musician. In their relationship Jones found the warm, nurturing father/son camaraderie that he had always craved.

> Brian and John shared a zealous fascination with British trams [at that time disappearing fast], John being a member of the Tramway Museum Society. (10, 1994)

This ties in with his subsequent love of trains that he revealed to Nick Broomfield. It was something about the fact that they were both rolling stock, limited by rails but offering, in their furthest reaches, a sense of adventure. I remember standing on Quainton Road station in Buckinghamshire, the long closed-down section of the Great Central and, despite the weeds and that only one side of track remained, you could look towards the distant blue hills and wonder what lay beyond that horizon. You could describe it as a sort of railway romance, reflected in the popular GWR posters of the time. The same internal response obviously had an effect on the young Jones.

John Appleby held in check the wilder extremes of his young friend, at least for the moment. But it seems there was never any time or place when Jones could entirely throw off the triple temptations of drink, drugs and women. So in considering the more beneficial aspects of Andrews and Appleby on Jones, I am rather less than convinced by the earlier rationale put forward that Jones' more extreme behaviour could be put down to epilepsy. It does not seem to entirely excuse him. There must have been something else, perhaps forever unexplained, in the mix that made up his extraordinary hyper character.

The problem now was that Brian, unsupported by Lewis, needed to earn some real money and, partly to try and please his parents, he put in for some (as it turned out short-lived) jobs starting, some might say laughably, as a bus conductor. However, having a fascination with buses and trams is not the same as getting up extremely early on cold winter mornings and working long hours in draughty buses, where you were always on your feet. As Giuliano tells us, this job lasted just three weeks.

Unable to take the strain at home, Jones was kindly offered accommodation with Patricia Andrews' sister and her husband, Bernie Taylor. This was an early example of Brian's billeting at the homes of his girlfriends, taking advantage of their parents and then making the girls pregnant before moving on without a backward glance. Anything not to be at home. There then followed a series of dead-end jobs including coal-man, factory worker and sales assistant, some lasting only days. Finally, Jones made an effort to make himself respectable in the eyes of his parents. His academic record, because of his obvious ability, was remarkable and should have been more than sufficient to guarantee him a place in The Cheltenham School of Architecture and in due course he applied and was accepted. However, a couple of days later, the offer was strangely withdrawn, apparently because,

> … he took a post as junior assistant with the architects' department
> of Gloucestershire County Council. Jones was showing real promise
> until he charmed a friend into footing the bill for a £30 overcoat,
> never repaying the debt. A trait that, not coincidentally, spilled over
> to several missed payments on his rent. (11, 1994)

Bernie, as Jones' landlord, incensed at the loss of £30, not to mention the rent, rather meanly advised the school's principal that what they had taken on,

> … was, in fact, 'An irresponsible drifter and potentially poor
> student.' (11, 1994)

This resulted in him being discarded, just when it looked as if he might have turned a corner. He was also allegedly banned from the school due to his continuous womanizing. Again, just not acceptable in good old Cheltenham. Bernie Taylor had become justifiably angered by Jones' behaviour and clearly regarded him as a cuckoo in the nest. So what appeared to be the ideal candidate with perfect qualifications changed overnight into an unreliable loser. He lost not only the post, but also his bolthole in Taylor's house. It was back to square one and back to his parents. You would think that this lesson might have convinced Jones to treat people more honourably. No such luck!

He could not throw off his inherent irresponsibility and most of the jobs he had taken in one last desperate attempt to appease his parents. Unfortunately, this series of dead-end jobs just seemed to aggravate the situation. Jones could not stick at anything and was sacked from most of the jobs he had taken on. During one of them Brian had a car accident, injuring his leg and losing a tooth. It was midwinter 1960 and Pat Andrews had to look after him. As Giuliano says, if it were not for this,

> … she might never have got a look at the Jones family.

> She recalls being led through a spotless and sterile house where a formidable atmosphere crackled tensely through the polite veneer of its occupants. 'I was reminded of a Victorian household, with its very sombre, very serious, foreboding atmosphere,' describes Andrews. 'There was no joy, no laughter, no happiness, nothing I knew at my own home.' …

> 'It was the middle of winter and she [Louisa] had done cucumber sandwiches and cake. Here Brian had just lost his tooth and had it screwed back in and she was doing up a tea as if nothing had happened. All I could think of was Brian feeling like death and his bloody, aching mouth.' (11/12, 1994)

The cucumber sandwiches seem to sum up all that was wrong with the Jones family, all show and no substance. But, above all, there seemed to be no sense of care and the whole family seemed devoid of emotion. Even Andrews' natural sympathy turned out to be misplaced.

Things went from bad to worse when Louisa Jones found out that Pat worked in Boots and her father worked at the same company as Lewis, Dowry Rotel, but on the shop floor. From that moment it became obvious

Semi-Detached Suburban Mr Jones

that Jones' parents thought Pat Andrews and her family highly unsuitable for her son. Simply not the right background, you know! At the same time, Lewis kept Brian's sister, Barbara, well apart from Brian, even to the extent of making them occupy different rooms in daytime. Though this is not fully explained, one can only imagine that Louisa did not want Barbara to be infected by the loose living virus that had apparently overwhelmed her son. The feeling of rejection that Brian felt was all too real and one can, to some extent, understand him kicking against this. He couldn't stand the claustrophobic atmosphere in the parental home and spent as much time away from it as possible, often with Dick Hattrell, whose home offered a far warmer and pleasanter space to be. Brian struck up a good relationship with Hattrell's father and found common ground on a variety of subjects from cricket to literature. Brian was, surprisingly, remarkably well read, in part because it was something he could do without dependence on anybody else. Not only did he have a good understanding of classical literature, but he had also read large sections of the Bible. This is particularly surprising given his chosen lifestyle.

Matters came to a head one day when, returning home for a change of a clothes, Brian found a suitcase stashed in the bushes outside his house with a note saying his parents had gone on holiday. While some of his things were in the case, there were others that he desperately needed inside the house so he broke in through the French window. Unfortunately, and you couldn't make this up, he was spotted by the neighbours who immediately called the police, thinking he was a burglar. This marked the end of Jones' life at his parents' home and, according to Giuliano, he moved into a small flat with his trusted friend, Dick Hattrell, the first of many such moves.

However, things went from bad to worse when it was discovered, that at just 16, Pat Andrews was expecting his third illegitimate child. Moving in to the tiny flat, Andrews may have had thoughts from their previous conversations that she would be able to stabilize the temperament of the mercurial Jones but while he initially appeared to value the child, Julian Mark, he soon reverted to type and all the misplaced confidence that Andrews had in him evaporated when he continued his philandering, gave her a black eye in an argument and turned his mind back to his one true interest, music. The

The Ties That Bind

lack of care in Brian's parents was also completely lacking in him. It must have been devastating for her. He also waited to grab her wages from Boots at the end of the week, often leaving her to go hungry. The common ground between them not unnaturally disappeared and she soon lost him physically as well. Andrews was a very ordinary and unexceptional teenager but she had established a relationship with Jones. It seems that the birth of the baby is what finally turned him against her. There was certainly a streak of ruthlessness in him and it should be obvious by now that, in any relationship, it was always Brian Jones who came first and nobody else mattered. It must have been a dreadful blow to her and one that remained with her for the rest of her life. At first she thought it was a temporary problem but Brian was by now in another flat and mixing with the great and the good of blues music. In an effort to move on, he struck up a relationship with Alexis Korner and his rhythm and blues band.

Brian became deeply fascinated by the intensely earthy and primitive music output of this group that he first encountered at The Ealing Jazz Club and he spent hours discussing its content with Korner. This is where he wanted to put all his pent-up energy. Jones was allowed to join the band and immediately impressed them with his ability on slide guitar, a notoriously difficult instrument to play. But there was something else as well attached to Brian beside his innate musical skill. It was charisma, and the kids who watched him play became increasingly aware of this. He was just a natural musical star, no matter what instrument he was playing. No wonder Pat Andrews and the baby no longer figured in his life. Music was everything to Brian and when Korner took him under his wing, the latter was immediately impressed by the way, musically speaking, he could take his audience along with him. According to Giuliano:

> 'He had a way of talking that was all his own,' grinned Korner. 'It was a beautiful mixture of good manners and rudeness. No one really knew very much about Brian's home life because he was very careful not to involve his escape route – music – with the middle class he was escaping.' (15, 1994)

Pat tried to recover the relationship but it was by this time hopeless as Brian was already mixing with blues stars like Chuck Berry and Bo Diddley.

Semi-Detached Suburban Mr Jones

> Pat, suddenly seeing it all slipping away, made one last desperate attempt to salvage the relationship. She packed up [Julian] Mark, took a bus to London and showed up at Brian's Notting Hill doorstep at 3 a.m.

> The move was to prove disastrous. Jones was now circling in another orbit … while Pat sat all but ignored in a corner. When Brian did pay her attention he often erupted in jealous tantrums forcing her to quit a number of jobs over some imagined infidelity. (15, 1994)

Exactly how long she was with him is unclear but it became more than obvious to her, as to everyone else in attendance, that all the pretty girls Brian paraded in front of her were an obvious sign that Brian, despite the birth of a child, wanted nothing else to do with the plain, practical but reliable Andrews. It was the ultimate insult.

Along with this new musical success came the usual hangers-on in the shape of endless young female groupies, some underage, and a new hard-edged cockiness. The early good manners, innocence and charm had all but disappeared and in its place was a rather nasty individual, devoid of any concern for others and just out for what he could get.

> It wasn't just the endless string of disposable dollybirds tucked under his arm, like the fourteen-year-old schoolgirl he openly paraded about town; nor the snazzy Italian box-jacket and winklepicker shoes he had purchased from her wages while she'd gone hungry. This was rather a new confidence, cocky, steely … He dropped his name, now calling himself [briefly it has to be said] Elmo Jones after his latest blues idol, Elmore James. (15, 1994)

The shallowness was one thing but his mental cruelty to Pat and others was quite extraordinary. In short, he was a complete bastard entirely devoted to promoting himself.

Andrews made a wasted trip to Brian's parents' house, believing that her father was getting the rough end of Lewis Jones' gossip at work. In the reaction she got, she finally realized that the haughty behaviour of Jones senior had re-emerged in the son. Lewis also seemed to have absolutely no concern for the way that she had been treated. So she finally left Brian,

The Ties That Bind

just leaving a note. He couldn't have cared less. He never showed any real concern for her or the baby and she realized that with his temperament, he would probably never be able to make any lasting relationship with the opposite sex or be able to rely more than temporarily on a male friend. And, frankly, he didn't deserve to.

But if his personal relationships were a disaster, elsewhere he was seen as a rising star and, as such, began to call the shots. That was all that mattered to him and where his pent-up energy was directed. Other young musicians, seeing his potential, wanted to play alongside him, presumably in the hope that some of the stardust would rub off on them. Just as with women, Brian picked and chose ruthlessly. The only thing that mattered was how he would be seen and appreciated. He was a deeply unattractive character, who eventually paid the price for his treatment of others and as Giuliano says:

> Years later, while Jones was earning a £1000 a week as a Rolling Stone and not contributing a penny to his son [or indeed the welfare of any of the other babies he had sired], Andrews had this to say: 'The one thing I feel badly about is when I'm walking down the road and Mark sees some toy and I can't afford to get it for him. I say to myself, Brian's got enough money, why can't he buy him something? But I never hear from him.' (16, 1994)

This seems a remarkably mild reaction, given what happened to her but, even now and despite his later success, she still felt sorry for a man who hit her and was quite incapable of making proper friends and that the people who gathered round him did so because of his skills, not his behaviour.

It is worth noting, musically speaking, that this was probably one of the few times in his life when he showed any real sense of purpose. Later on, after he had consumed too many drugs and too much drink, he lost that ability to make worthwhile decisions and progress. So, from the foregoing, we can see exactly how Jones became sufficiently influential and jockeyed himself into position to found The Rolling Stones and to pick and choose its members. At the height of Jones' conceit, according to Giuliano, he was heard to say:

Semi-Detached Suburban Mr Jones

I don't join other people's groups ... people join mine. (16, 1994)

One might say that at this point he was at his peak as a mover and shaker and that everything that happened afterwards started him on a slow downward spiral.

The Rolling Stones were founded in 1962 with their work unsurprisingly rooted in the blues music that Brian Jones had taken on so assiduously, but also took some account of the current popularity of rock and roll which they had to do to remain popular. Mick Jagger was taken on as singer and Keith Richards as guitarist, bassist Bill Wyman, drummer Charlie Watts with Jones himself as a multi-instrumentalist. At first they didn't make a great deal of money and were more widely known as iconic of the counterculture revolution seen in a rather more gentle form in the Woodstock, NY music festival. Only later did Jagger and Richards tool their blues-influenced rock and roll to a more commercial end. But Jagger and Richards also developed something that Jones lacked, a continued determination to steer the group towards commercial success and, while they may have started as inferior musicians to Jones, they quickly learned the ropes while Brian became ever more frequently quixotic, showing an undisciplined attitude towards the group and importantly, a failure to lead it. Brian's failure to connect with his parents seemed to be at the root of all his difficulties but simply cannot be regarded as an acceptable excuse for his poor behaviour.

> Cheltenham ... remained a place filled with emotional scars that would haunt him forever after. At the height of his popularity and fame as a Rolling Stone, he and chauffeur Brian Palastanga stopped for a rare visit home. Palastanga remembers a warm summer evening on the front lawn, talking with Lewis Jones when he happened to look up and see Brian standing at the bedroom window peering out wistfully, a veritable little boy lost. (17, 1994)

So while the hard-edged Brian Jones was uppermost in his ruthless desire to use his skills to get to the top, underneath it there was still the middle-class boy from Cheltenham, forever searching for what he had lost. I believe it was this aspect that eventually led him to purchase Cotchford Farm, along with its connections. When the money and the empty trappings of success

The Ties That Bind

no longer seemed so important, all that was left was the possibility of trying to regain his middle-class respectability. The problem was that he already destroyed in a few short years any possibility of realizing that dream. His behavioural problems had already had serious repercussions for many of those with whom he came in contact, especially the girls. It is to their credit that some of them managed to get over it and rebuild their lives while, strangely, still holding a candle for the errant Jones. He was nothing if not charismatic, but he was also an empty shell.

SPOTLIGHT:
THE ILLEGITIMATE CAST-OFFS

This list cites the five illegitimate children sired by Brian Jones that we can be definite about. Some sources suggest there may be six or even seven. Brian's teenage Scandinavian sojourn when banished by his parents could have been a source for more but only the following have been confirmed. As you can see, it was pretty much an annual event.

(1) Barry David (1959) with Valerie Corbett. Given up for adoption.
(2) Belinda (1960) with Angeline who was married at the time.
(3) Julian Mark (1961) with Patricia Andrews.
(4) Julian Brian (1964) with Linda Lawrence.
(5) John (Paul Andrew) (1965) with Dawn Molloy. Adopted.

These children, for whom a basic one-off settlement was made, would not have been entitled to anything by law. Up until then The Poor Act 1575 formed the basis of English bastardy law. It existed to punish a bastard child's mother and putative father, and to relieve the parish from the cost of supporting mother and child. The Legitimacy Act of 1926 relented on this if the parents were to later marry. The 'bastards' law' of 1969, ironically the year of Brian Jones' death, changed all that and gave later illegitimate children some entitlement to recognition and financial compensation. The number of children born to Brian in this way could probably only be bettered by straying royalty over the centuries. However, from what we know, the hardship and heartache these women and their offspring encountered can only be guessed at. Certainly, Brian's lack of responsibility was as remarkable as it was despicable. However, despite the sadness and the hardship, I am struck by the determination of these families to survive and, surprisingly, not always to condemn their errant father.

An account of John, born to Dawn Molloy, appears in a *Spotlight* section later in the book.

THE STONE AGE

It is not the remit of this book to follow the well trammelled path in recounting the history of The Rolling Stones but it is worth noting that Brian Jones' membership lasted all of an increasingly problematic seven years, from 1962–1969. During this time Jones was very much responsible for honing the American-influenced blues sound that made The Stones a successful group. His ability with different instruments was legendary but unfortunately so was his drinking, drug taking and womanizing. He garnered a well-deserved bad reputation even within a world where bad behaviour was often the norm, so although the group initially prospered under him, he totally failed to see that his antics and his lack of leadership would eventually be responsible for his downfall.

Mick Jagger and Keith Richards had first come across Brian Jones at the same Ealing jazz club frequented by Alexis Korner. Giuliano recounts how:

> 'They were very much in awe of him,' friend 'Spanish' Tony Sanchez recalled in *Up and Down with the Rolling Stones*: 'It wasn't just that his musical knowledge and ability dwarfed theirs, it was their thinly concealed envy for the fact that he lived dangerously and walked firmly on the wild side of life, while they combined rebellion with a cosy life at home with mum and dad.' (19, 1994)

Brian Jones had by this time bolted on to his cockiness an alluring sexual appeal which, despite his short stature, he employed whenever he wanted to attract the attention of whoever he was talking to. It was in the way he moved and in the flick of his blonde mop and, if looked at now, it might seem ridiculous, at the time it was instrumental in drawing in the talents of Jagger and Richards into the band. It was also initially responsible for luring, at least initially, the beautiful German/Italian Anita Pallenberg who, for a while at least, became his most notable girlfriend. However, she was made of sterner stuff than the average groupie and eventually, once established, she began to weave her magic on the whole group. If Jones was manipulative, so was she but in a far more controlled and far-sighted way. What she did was mostly coldly effective and she saw through clear foreign eyes exactly how the inexperienced Jagger and Richards had been taken in by the peacock, almost camp, display of the (at this time) influential Jones.

> Jones patiently taught him [Jagger] the fundamentals of blues harmonica despite his blatant disrespect for singers who weren't musicians. They were also similarly drawn together by some early recordings made at IBC Studios in Portland Place. (20, 1994)

Eventually, having learned from the master, Jagger then bided his time but eventually fought hard to take over the group from Jones. So whilst Jagger/ Richards wanted to be more commercial and move away from the pure blues sound patented by Jones, many of their songs still contained a blues influence. He, of course, succeeded but now, more than 50 years later, it seems that Jones' highly influential, if rumbustious, years with the group have almost been expunged from history and many regard The Rolling Stones as always having been Jagger's group. Some are surprised to learn that it was not always the case because, as the years have rolled on, Jagger's leadership seems to be the natural default, albeit highly successful.

After setting the scene I want to concentrate on the process that gradually wrecked the relationship between Jones and the other band members and what led him to seek peace and tranquillity at Cotchford Farm. But, amid all the allegations about Jones, there is one aspect of him we should always remember. It was his incredible ability on a range of musical instruments and his charisma whilst performing that helped establish the unique sound of The Rolling Stones. The girls adored him even if their parents didn't. But, perhaps to the chagrin of the rest of the group, it was his star quality that initially led the way. His music may have made him but, as a human being, he was totally directionless. It wasn't that the other Stones behaved like saints. They certainly didn't.

> Keith [Richards], particularly, talked about fights he'd been in and things he'd shoplifted, but even he couldn't hide his shock when Brian casually mentioned his worry over [at the time] two illegitimate children. (19, 1994)

The Stone Age

Theirs was a more working-class background than Brian's. It's just that Brian went so much further than the rest and, despite everything, had a relatively commanding way of speaking. He somehow pulled you in and grabbed your attention, even when some of it was just so much bullshit. The other Stones, at first naïve and, relatively speaking, schoolboys, were totally in awe of this young man who was so supremely musically capable and so certain of himself. In this, surely, were born the seeds of envy that, when the time was right, would find Brian thrown out of his own band.

> The early relationship between Jagger and Jones was certainly one of hero worship on the part of the younger, more inexperienced Mick. Jagger idolised Jones for his ability to read music, his accomplished musicianship, and mostly, for those goading, slightly effeminate displays Brian threw off on stage. Jones patiently taught him the fundamentals of blues harmonica despite his blatant disrespect for singers who weren't musicians. (20, 1994)

But the trouble with being cocksure of yourself is that, eventually, you are riding towards a fall.

> As Marianne Faithfull observed: 'Although in the end, Mick became intent on replacing Brian [as leader], in the beginning, Brian was, in effect, his role model.' (20, 1994)

So, despite their other faults and their history, Mick Jagger and Keith Richards were eventually more grounded, more organized and more ambitious in their determination to succeed than the increasingly wild Jones with his inability for self-discipline. Yet at the beginning he was still considerably more effective, 'relentlessly soliciting investors and badgering club owners to give the Stones a chance.' (20, 1994) And he needed to because, together with Jagger and friend Dick Hattrell, they were living in,

> … a two-room bedsit in Edith Grove, Chelsea, a rat-infested dump without working plumbing and only a few naked light bulbs that operated via an electric coin meter. (20, 1994)

The rent was £7 a week which came largely from Jagger's LSE grant supplemented by Jones working as a shop assistant at Whiteley's department store. I have no doubt that Jagger was the main contributor but it seems ironic when comparing this bastion of respectability (Whiteley's) with the kind of life these two were leading at the time. There was also a certain amount of thieving going on with Jones dipping his hand into the till more than once and even nicking neighbours' empty bottles so that they could retrieve the deposit on them. That indicates a certain desperation. Jones was also not above stealing from his colleagues if the opportunity presented itself. He had no scruples whatsoever. Dick Hattrell, their flatmate, had unexpectedly received a cheque for £80 from his time in the Territorial Army.

> Jones first whipped the sweater off his back and handed it to a shivering Keith while taking Hattrell's coat for himself. He then not only snatched the entire pay cheque for food and booze, but bought himself a spanking new guitar as well. (20, 1994)

Whilst accepting that financial controls were less strict in the 1960s, Giuliano fails to explain how Jones was able to appropriate the cheque. However, this in no way detracts from the fact that Jones could be a thoroughly reprehensible individual in many ways, combining his musical skills with many of the facets of a con man. He even stole money from Richards' pocket while he slept. It seems hard to believe that this Cheltenham educated boy was such a complete scoundrel.

Jones' paramount concern was keeping the band together but, around this time, Mick Jagger seemed more uncertain about continuing. An accountant's career was beckoning him, especially as it meant regular money and not having to live in a parlous state in the Edith Grove flat. Because of this, Jones thought that if that happened, Keith Richards would also leave as he was a close friend of Jagger from the same area of Dartford. Whereas Jones was indifferent about Jagger, he thought it was essential that he hang on to Keith Richards whose skill he valued more. So he hatched a cunning plan. While Jagger was away during the day at college, he decided to enhance his relationship with Richards as much as possible. There was a certain commonality. Both of their fathers were engineers although Keith, due to an almighty row, did not speak to his father for around 20 years. This chimed with the falling out of Jones with his own parents. Apart from that, Jones decided to major on encouraging Keith towards that special Stones sound

The Stone Age

which involved, *inter alia*, the concept of running two guitars together to create that special blues sound. This plan worked wonderfully well for a while with Keith getting significantly closer to Jones and Jagger starting to feel decidedly left out. Apart from anything else, it was one way to keep warm in their decidedly downmarket hovel. As a result, Jagger began to become ever more resentful.

> In Jones's obsessive desire to achieve, anyone was expendable. Predictably, the first on his list was the ever malleable Dick Hattrell, with his dubious position as band roadie. The bespectacled 5′3″, rotund rock wannabe followed Brian like a lapdog. Jones however, wanting to distance himself from anything remotely close to his provincial roots, always made Hattrell walk a respectful ten yards behind. (21, 1994)

Hattrell was often made to stump up for meals at the local Wimpy Bar and sometimes deliberately shut out of the flat all night. When there was no more money to be had, Jones sadistically attempted to get rid of him; first by stripping him and then, unbelievably, trying to electrocute him. Even after shutting him out completely, Hattrell always remained a ridiculously loyal friend to Jones. What is interesting here is that given Jones' skill at manipulating people, it seems odd that towards the end of his short life he became the victim rather than the perpetrator, at the hands of other even more skilled manipulators. This may be because he became an alcoholic and that the wild living had begun to take its toll. At this point you may also be asking if we should care about such a person and yet in some strange way we do. This may be partly because of his celebrity combined with an indefinable vulnerability which, despite his appalling behaviour, occasionally comes to the surface.

When Nick Broomfield found himself sharing a railway carriage with Brian Jones as described earlier in this book, he revealed that he was interested in both trams and trains. Adam Sweeting reports it as follows:

> But perhaps what really tickled Broomfield's filmmaking fancy was not a fascination with vintage rolling stock, but the way Jones personified the generation gap that yawned at the beginning of the

45

1960s … His father noted how Brian underwent a 'peculiar change' in his early teens and embarked on a lifestyle of playing in blues clubs, often surviving by billeting himself on the families of a string of girlfriends. The girlfriends frequently ended up becoming pregnant. (42, 2023)

Brian also developed a reputation as a cruel prankster, behaviour that was not confined to his flatmates.

Kathy Etchingham, most noted for her high profile relationship with Jimi Hendrix, was subject to many a twisted prank. 'He did some bloody evil things to me. We went to this party together and he told me that the drinks were in the garage. So I went marching back there. What he didn't tell me was there was a big hole in the floor and I went straight into it. He thought it was very funny. I had no skin on my knees and elbows. He was behind me when I walked in and brought a few friends to watch.' Little wonder that Jones didn't endear himself to many people. (22, 1994)

And so the desire to destroy, to break up, that had at first appeared as a child continued into his life as an adult.

The band gradually began to become more successful and develop a following in Ealing yet, strangely, Jones still wanted to obtain parental approval. Why he should think like that given what had gone before is surprising.

'To me,' said the elder Jones, 'this was evidence that in spite of our early disagreements he still regarded me as his confidant. He came to Cheltenham to see us and was full of ambition for the future … From that moment on there was a complete and lasting reconciliation.' (22, 1994)

However, this seems unduly simplistic if not downright untrue. The classically trained parents were always unable and, indeed, unwilling to accept the attraction of jazz and blues music and, as such, could never reconcile themselves with Brian. According to Keith Richards, Jones would often spend hours writing and rewriting missives to his parents in order to win them over. And subsequent visits demonstrated that the gap between them was as wide as ever. What he wanted from them was a seal of approval and, sadly, despite his father's assertion, he never got it. This is unsurprising given Brian's recent history of spreading his seed far and wide.

But Broomfield, whilst making his documentary *The Stones and Brian Jones* made a fascinating discovery. The title suggests that Jones has always been an outsider, from the group that he founded, from his family and indeed from many other people with whom he came in contact. Broomfield found a lost letter from Brian's father containing a poignant apology for his failure to comprehend or accept him for what he was and asking for forgiveness. He does not say exactly when this was written but it could have been after Brian's death when the full force of what had happened hit him.

> 'I have been a very poor and intolerant father in many ways,' he [Lewis Jones] wrote. (43, 2023)

Broomfield goes on to suggest that people who were born before World War II had a different view of the world from those who were, like Brian, born after it because,

> … the world changed so much in that time and there was such a generational conflict. (43, 2023)

This seems something of a generalization and seems to apply most specifically to the Jones family and the term 'conflict', although applicable in Brian's case would not have been replicated in every case despite the very real changes. What Lewis was totally unable to understand was Brian's need to kick against the accepted and very comfortable way of life that had been provided for him. Summarized, it was contempt for the status quo.

According to Giuliano:

> Jones' girlfriend at the time, Linda Lawrence, claimed Brian's parents totally ignored him and that it was only after he'd made a successful record they even acknowledged his birthday. 'The contact was because he had made it, money,' affirmed Lawrence, 'but that wasn't the contact he was looking for.' [He wanted parental approval.] Later incidents would also contest Lewis Jones's declaration of restored father/son harmony. (23, 1994)

Semi-Detached Suburban Mr Jones

With his background Jones could afford to play the middle-class bohemian while Jagger and Richards, at best from a lower suburban background, were regarded by Jones as somehow inferior. At the beginning Jones really knew how to attract the crowds and the girls with a carefully honed performance designed to draw you in. In effect, it was all a stage act but it fooled audiences everywhere probably because, despite being diminutive, he had this fantastic charisma which, when combined with his musical ability, was irresistible. According to Alexis Korner:

> Brian was the aggressive member of The Stones. He'd do that funny tiptoe dance of his, right to the edge of the stage and slap the tambourine in the audience's face as if to say, "F**k you!" then he'd drop back again, leering at you all the time so as to make you really angry. (23, 1994)

> Cream percussionist, Ginger Baker, … remembers Jones as a born performer right from the beginning … 'I noticed that Mick just stood at the mike, almost motionless, and sang. It was Brian who was the showman, leaping about, playing on his knees and running into the crowd with his guitar. When you went to see The Stones in the early days Brian was the one you wanted to see.' (24, 1994)

He was the star. But there was another side to it, as described by journalist Judith Simonds. We have to remember that Jones suffered from asthma and these attacks would happen maybe three times a week. As a result he was terrified that one of these would occur while he was on stage, leading him to break down mid-performance. This caused him substantial anxiety and even panic. So, as some sort of counter to this, he developed an aggressive, snarling performance that wilfully tried to exclude the possibility of this happening. Said Simonds:

> 'Through his asthma, stage work was agony for him. Working to counteract his fear of an attack he promoted the most unsmiling, violent image of the group.' (24, 1994)

And yet somehow it all worked and through it all he managed to create a charisma that Jagger and the other members of the group could only dream of. But change was on the way, and it was this that began to eat into his position as leader and the absolute authority.

The Stone Age

In May 1963, The Rolling Stones signed a much-needed management agreement with Andrew Loog Oldham, whom Jones disliked on sight. Despite this, he managed to secure a private deal which meant an extra £5 per week for him personally and, despite its supposed confidentiality, it eventually leaked out and began to cause a bubbling resentment among the other members. It may not seem much to us now but at the time it was a worthwhile sum of money. Brian should have treated everyone equally but he was just too greedy. At the time the group consisted of six members which Oldham, probably quite rightly, thought was too many to be effective. As a result Ian Stewart, a burly pianist, turned up one day and was hustled towards the exit. Brian Jones, in true style, promised that he would still receive a one-sixth share of the takings but, of course, he never did. Oldham said that, apart from anything else, he just didn't physically look the part which was undoubtedly true. Stewart was very hurt by this but he, for a while at least, continued as part of the band in the guise of road manager, the role recently vacated by the inept Dick Hattrell. However, the brutality of his dismissal stung.

The other part of Oldham's management team was Eric Easton. He may not have played such an important part in organizing the group as Oldham but he came up with an idea, ultimately unrealized, that suited Brian Jones perfectly. Easton wanted to exit Jagger from the group on the basis that his singing voice was weak and that he seemed uncomfortable outside the strict blues format. This would have meant the removal of a potential rival as well as giving Brian the opportunity to bring in the superior, in his view, Paul Jones, later with Manfred Mann, to come in as lead vocalist. Brian had always seen himself as back-up vocalist but he simply wasn't up to it. His skills lay with all the different instruments he could play. In the event, Jagger remained intact because Oldham overruled Easton but something had to be done to make him more effective and this came with training; improved harmonica technique and a more lively stage persona. From then on Jagger was made. There was always an imbalance between Jagger/Richards and Jones and it eventually came to a head in June 1969 at Cotchford Farm. Somehow the three of them, despite Brian's best efforts, just never seemed to gel.

Semi-Detached Suburban Mr Jones

In the meantime, Brian, according to his usual behaviour of taking advantage of others, had moved in with his then girlfriend Linda Lawrence and her family in comfortable Windsor, and a subtle shift in the power base began which was never later corrected. Jagger and Richards had left the one-horse flat at Edith Grove and moved in with Oldham, which proved even more divisive. All Brian's cosying up to Keith went for nothing and he re-established his relationship with Jagger. Absolute authority began to seep away from Jones towards Jagger and Richards, especially the former. Linda's father, Alex, accompanied Brian and Linda on trips to Oldham's office and Brian took against him immediately. He was very obviously siding with Richards and Jagger, the latter always jealous of Jones. Jagger wanted to be top cat and after Brian's death he always was, although the recent photos of an 80-plus-year-old trying to party like someone 60 years younger are surprising. He even had a minder nearby to ensure he remained secure. But by this time, of course, it was as if Brian Jones had never existed.

One explanation for this is quite simple. In any group it is the singer who gets most audience attention and the spotlight always shines brighter on them than any of the others. Two other things had happened. Jagger had learned fast from Jones, and Jones' charisma, once the leading attraction in the group, had begun to fade. Jagger, once so static, began to move round the stage in a much more stylish fashion, almost stolen from the master himself. The girl groupies, initially attracted to the middle-class Jones were, on actually meeting with him, alarmed by his unpredictability and wild behaviour. He almost seemed like a threat. As a result they began to turn towards Jagger as a more interesting influence.

> Jagger learned how small, tantalising body movements could tease
> up conventional screams to a banshee-like howl. He began to slip off
> his Cecil Gee jacket and dangle it on his forefinger like a stripper's
> G-string. (26, 1994)

All of this was picked up by the manipulative Oldham whose loyalty remained with Jagger and it wasn't long before he started putting it about deliberately that Jones was receiving £5 more than the others. This naturally caused even more resentment, as it was intended to do, since the others felt it could be more profitably spent on other things. This was all part of the whispering campaign that Oldham organized to pull the carpet from under Jones. And nothing turned out rougher than the moment in The Cavern Club, on The Beatles' home territory, when the rest of the group found out about Brian's extra £5 a week. It was at this point that Keith Richards really let it be known about his reservations about Brian as leader. And when, at the Southend Odeon, it was found that Brian had consumed Keith's chicken dinner, he ended up with a black eye. His filching had gone too far.

Brian Jones did not help himself by feigning superiority over the others and, where there was a choice, taking the best options for himself. Brian's selfishness had come home to roost. He was not a natural leader, just a noisy one and he didn't command the necessary respect from the other members of the group. In fact, just as he had done in the past with others, he often treated them with contempt. On top of that Brian began to obviously suffer from a range of ailments on top of his asthma, so much so that he began to miss some of the shows. This had a disastrous effect.

> He was on constant medication for back problems, ear infections, sore throats, and frequently came away from health clinics diagnosed with 'nervous strain'. 'Brian's illnesses became a band joke,' said Wyman. 'Mick and Keith would say sarcastically, "Oh, Brian's ill again, does he have a doctor's certificate?" He seemed a hypochondriac and when you're young you haven't time for other people's illnesses.' (27, 1994)

So just as The Stones under Oldham's direction began to achieve stardom, Brian's authority started to wane. Being of short stature also did not help. What he wanted was incredibly shallow. He wanted to impress people with his sports car, his performance on stage, his musicality, the latest clothing and his appearances in magazines. It was an instantaneous recognition which ultimately died in the bud. He wanted to be admired and loved by all but Brian's behaviour demonstrated repeatedly that he was not a loveable individual.

> Linda Lawrence maintains that Brian's behaviour stemmed from an absolute need to be a celebrity [and we should take into account his attempts at showing off as a child and at school. It never left him.]

Semi-Detached Suburban Mr Jones

> 'He felt he had to be a star because he [most certainly] was not a star in his family … It wasn't his ego. It was something he wanted to fulfil, that he hadn't got from his childhood.' (27, 1994)

But he had a curious way of going about it, playing dangerous pranks on Linda such as taking her on boat rides where he would lurch close to a waterfall, driving her into a deserted forest at night and locking all the car doors while menacing her, which seems quite extraordinary. She underwent close to physical abuse from Brian and it is a wonder that her father did not have something to say about it.

Nevertheless Brian took Linda to introduce her to his parents.

> He considered her the right sort of girl to gain their approval. She was a quiet, well-mannered and frightfully middle-class county girl. "The visit was a disaster," Linda recalled. "Brian's parents made it clear that there was still little he could do in their opinion to amend their sheer disappointment in him. Hardly a word was spoken. Even when Brian suggested that they and his parents go out to a pub in order to liven up the proceedings, the atmosphere didn't change."

> It was as if Brian didn't exist. It hurt Brian terribly because he so wanted to reach them. He tried to get them to listen to his music but that didn't help. Even his sister [Barbara] was discouraged from taking an interest. (49, 2016)

Then Brian had insisted that Linda Lawrence accompany him on the Arden tour in 1963 but this caused further upheaval and a bad atmosphere in the band when the other girls wondered why they hadn't been selected.

> 'I never felt he was cruel,' notes Linda curiously, 'but rather releasing something hurtful from his past that made him angry.' (27, 1994)

Despite her surprisingly forgiving reaction, this was almost certainly the truth; relating of course to the constant rejection by his own family, a fact that, throughout his life, he could never get over. But to me his behaviour seems quite unforgivable, especially when Linda gave birth to (yet another) illegitimate child, Julian, and whom, just as he had done before,

The Stone Age

Brian soundly rejected and refused to take any responsibility for. We might have expected Linda's parents to throw him out but curiously and, despite his behaviour, they were hugely fond of Brian and, presumably, hoped for wedding bells. Fat chance! Indeed, so used was he to this way of things, he didn't even bother to inform his parents and it was left to Linda's mother to address this deficiency. It was just another example of Brian using people who had been good to him and damn the consequences. You might imagine that they would have recognized that trait in him early on but Linda just became another sacrifice to Brian's overwhelming vanity. But the direction that Oldham was taking the band would prove to be his undoing, together with his increasingly wild behaviour combined with his illnesses. He was unable to control himself and this fact made him even more restless.

It was during this tour that the ever reliable Dick Hattrell made a reappearance after a period of illness. He found, surprisingly, he couldn't get near Brian in the Odeon theatre but then realized, since this was Cheltenham and home territory, he would probably be found in one of his favourite watering holes, in this case The Waikiki. Hattrell was amazed to discover Brian drinking strong liquor entirely alone, dressed in a big fur coat but with a haunted look on his face. His past was beginning to catch up with him. Whilst he perked up when Hattrell appeared, it was obvious that he was trying to drown his sorrows in vast quantities of booze. Alcoholism was on the horizon. There was also an inner loneliness.

In the meantime Andrew Oldham, generally a reliable source of what a group needed to succeed, made a completely wrong decision. Oldham saw The Stones as the natural successors to The Beatles and they were anything but; far more iconoclastic with a completely different range of music. While thinking along these mistaken lines, he wanted the band to effect conformity by wearing identical stage clothes.

> Their stage uniforms consisted of Cuban-heeled boots, black trousers and blue leather waistcoats, topped with the garish black and white dogtooth check jackets. (50, 2016)

This concept had been fitting for Brian Epstein's Beatles but it was a complete nonsense for The Stones. As a result, he found himself completely ignored when the band turned up to perform in their street clothes. For once Jones and Jagger found themselves on the same side. Oldham was predictably furious but calmed down when he began to realize that the press had a completely different view in which they regarded each member in turn as unique and that they dressed accordingly. The Stones were the complete antithesis of Epstein's group. One felt that The Beatles, as individuals, were probably nice and polite enough that you could easily introduce them to your parents. There was, apparently, a built-in element of conformity and good behaviour. The Stones were the complete opposite; very rough round the edges.

Having had some success with *Come On*, The Stones were looking for inspiration for a follow-up record but could not decide on it. Meanwhile Oldham accidentally found a solution. John Lennon and Paul McCartney spotted Oldham at a Variety Club award presentation.

> The pair sauntered over to him, only to hear about the unhappy manager's dilemma. Lennon offered a simple but generous solution to The Stones' problem. He said that the band could record a number they had written for their forthcoming album. Oldham couldn't believe his ears. He rushed the two Beatles back to the studio where all six Stones were staring blankly at their instruments. (51, 2016)

That song was *I Wanna Be Your Man* and was quickly and efficiently recorded by The Stones with Brian's significant Chicago blues feel giving it a very original edge for a UK record at that time. It may have been a Beatles song, but it was securely done in The Rolling Stones' style. From this we can also make another deduction. However clever Brian was with different instruments, it was the singer that usually got the attention. And that was Jagger.

The song also announced the debut of Nanker Phelge Publishing, set up to handle all songwriting and recordings by The Stones with the royalties accruing split evenly six ways, one part going to Oldham himself. This was the end of 1963 and was probably the point when the Stones became fully professional. It was also another nail in the coffin for Brian, who may have had on-stage charisma but lacked two important features. He had no

The Stone Age

obvious songwriting skills, essential for a group like The Stones, and he lacked the professionalism to continue to lead the band in the right direction. He had no meaningful vision of the future for the group.

At this point we should consider in more detail exactly what sort of problems Brian Jones had. He was not, for some reason, grounded in any form of reality and this created problems for him from a very early age. He had absolutely no moral compass and no anchor. It was as if the stiff and starchy parents from which he had sprung, Lewis and Louisa, had discovered a cuckoo in the nest. Coming so soon after the death of one daughter, they had no idea how to deal with him. All they did know is that they wanted to protect their other daughter, Barbara, from anything threatening and this unfortunately included Brian. In any event, Barbara seems a relatively shadowy figure who, when she grew up, could surely have made her own decisions about how to deal with such a wayward personality but there seems to have been little contact and, despite his wild side, the thing that Brian craved more than anything else was family approval. Sadly he never got it and this seemed to twist his behaviour even more. Also, despite having formed The Rolling Stones, Brian seemed to have no real idea how to run the group effectively and saving the best things for himself out of a sense of entitlement was not likely to go down well with the rest of the band. This feigned superiority had no basis in fact except in terms of his remarkable ability with different musical instruments. But that skill did not equate to leadership and once Andrew Oldham got control of the management, Brian's days as group leader were bound to be numbered.

Oldham was, at the very least, focussed and professional and the incidence of Brian's constant medical problems and bizarre behaviour were just the beginning of his slide from early power. The other Stones, particularly Jagger and Richards, were quick to learn the plus points from Jones while rejecting the other wholly unnecessary side of his character. Even his stage performance that so impressed the audience was copied in all but name by Jagger. Jones' unstable personality, however, really began to come to grief ironically as The Stones became more and more successful, moving from seedy lodgings towards big money and worldwide acclaim. They were, in many respects, a much more interesting group than the rather contained

Semi-Detached Suburban Mr Jones

Beatles. While they appeared iconoclastic to many, there were songs in their repertoire that were more romantic like *Lady Jane* and *Blue Turns to Grey*.

And this, of course, puts the finger on Brian's other failing; his complete inability to come up with any completed original songs which was surely an essential part of his leadership. He wrote his own poems which he tried to set to music but his efforts were puny compared with the songwriting skills of Jagger and Richards. The band needed a string of commercial pop songs and Brian was quite unable to provide this. So, despite being supremely clever in many other aspects of musicality, Brian failed dismally in the things that mattered to be able to lead the group. His was a wasted talent and a wasted life. Within the group he just did not concentrate on the things that that would promote it and instead went for the short-term option and the infantile desire to impress which simply didn't work. Even if the relationship with his parents had been solid, it seems doubtful if the outcome, in terms of his behaviour, would have changed that much. We shall probably never get to the bottom of why he behaved in such a wild manner but it is possible that the loss of one sister at such a young age had something to do with it. However, having reached maturity we might have expected more stability but there was none and that, combined with some terrible decision-making and several doses of bad luck, set what seemed then inevitable in motion. Everything about him just got worse.

By the time we reach 1964, it was clear that Brian wanted his own space and that was partly achieved by driving to gigs in the car belonging to Linda's parents with just her as passenger with the other Stones all crammed in the back of Stu's van. Quite why Brian continued to be so popular with Linda's father remains unclear, especially as the car suffered a number of regular bumps under Brian's erratic and sometimes drunken driving. It was an obvious marker for continuing resentment but Brian carried on regardless, blissfully unaware that his selfishness would eventually have dire consequences. It should also be noted that Andrew Oldham was no pushover, not even for Jagger and Richards.

By the time the second English tour got underway The Stones were getting close to the top of their game despite any ill feeling in the group and their first LP, simply entitled *The Rolling Stones* went straight to the top of the

56

The Stone Age

charts. A simple, sombre monochrome photo adorned the album and, apart from the Decca logo, there was no title or graphics. It was a risky venture but it paid off. And, according to Rawlings and Spendel, its style,

> … was implying that The Rolling Stones were bigger than the music they created. (53, 2016)

This was accompanied by the Lawrences' extraordinary decision to rename their house *Rolling Stone* in appreciation. When Brian first discovered this one night returning from work, he was completely bowled over. As the concerts got more and more popular, they also got more dangerous and Brian rightly advised Linda to stay clear of them for her own good. It is hard to quantify but there has always been a connection between successful rock stars and cheap crooks. It is a melting pot to which both sides seem attracted. There was often a mob at the theatre door and sometimes it got close to violence, even at The Savoy in genteel Cheltenham, and they only got away in one piece due to roadie Stu inventively backing the van right up to the stage doors. Such success bred similar events wherever they went but The Stones still kept up the frenetic pace. And so their second tour of their own country was an unbridled if not very disciplined success. All this had an effect on the brittle stability of Brian and Linda's relationship, not to mention their child; it became clear that their futures were going in different directions and that they could never live together permanently. But then that was what Brian was good at, breaking things up. And history just continued to repeat itself.

After splitting up with Linda and making a settlement towards her upkeep, Brian, never without a female for long, took up with Zouzou, a French model who, then, spoke virtually no English. But, apart from the obvious physical attraction, it did not last long because of the language barrier.

> "It took such a long time to say just one thing to each other," Brian morosely commented after they had split up. (63, 2016)

This could hardly have come as a surprise although she learned passable English in later years and has commented on the relationship.

And so the whole thing continued in a repetitious cycle until, in Munich, Brian was introduced to German/Italian model Anita Pallenberg. The difference here was that she was no pushover and she soon began to develop an influence over not only him, but also the rest of The Stones. But, this may also have been the time when Brian was introduced to drugs in a serious way, a habit, just like the girls and the booze, that he was unable to kick and which eventually landed him in a lot of trouble, both with the police and other members of the band. Pallenberg, recognizing his malleability, tempted him with hash. Rawlings and Spendel tell us that:

> Brian moved home again, this time to number one, Courtfield Road, South Kensington. His [previous] Elm Park mews flat had been receiving the regular, unfavourable interest of the local constabulary. The problem had arisen due to the flat's close proximity to the home of a well-known society doctor [not named!] who listed among his patients a large number of suspected drug users. (67, 2016)

Brian already had an unhealthy intake of legally prescribed substances but he also took quite a number that weren't. In short with his drinking, his drugs and his girls, he was an unholy mess. The doctor in question had apparently made a number of visits to Brian's home and the neighbours, for purely selfish reasons, had wasted no time in tipping off the law. So combined with the regular crowd of groupies outside the previous flat, the neighbours were extremely glad when Brian, reading the signs, moved to his new flat, just off Gloucester Road, South Kensington, and there installed the charismatic Anita Pallenberg. While she was with him, the balance of power began to change as she sought to influence him in a way no girlfriend before or since had done.

Just as before, Brian was soon in a full-blooded relationship with Anita, and past conquests like Linda were quickly forgotten. Linda's parents must have been disappointed in thinking that ever restless Jones would settle down and become a family man. Either they were not familiar with his previous history or they were just plain naïve. What must they have thought when Jones' ever more bizarre behaviour led to him being picked up by the police, not once but several times. Perhaps by then their eyes had cleared and they realized that Linda had had a relatively lucky escape. In a way Brian resembled a con man selling his wares, all shiny on the outside until you realized that what he was tempting you with was actually an empty

The Stone Age

basket. He was a liability, not only to himself, but to almost everyone with whom he came in contact. I am not suggesting for a minute that the other Stones always behaved well. They certainly didn't and the evidence, court records and otherwise, is there to prove it. It is just that they did not generally go to such extremes as to put the future of the band in jeopardy.

SPOTLIGHT:
JOHN (PAUL ANDREW) MOLLOY

At first the illegitimate children seemed to be an unwelcome footnote to the exploits of Brian Jones but the more I delved into it, I realized that there were a number of untold stories showing great determination amongst the sadness and their terrible start in life. At the time, 60 years ago, being an illegitimate child had more shock value than it does today and with it came the possibility of condemning them and their mothers quite as much as the errant Jones. But the children are to be pitied for no fault can attach to them and I came to admire just how well some of them had overcome this apparent handicap. None more so than John, son of Dawn Molloy, who in telling his tale to Scott Jones of the *Daily Mail* reveals a poignancy in coming from the wrong side of the tracks and doing rather well.

> The black car always came on a Wednesday to take the newborn babies away from the home for unmarried mothers. Nobody would speak. People kept out of the way. Then, afterwards, you would hear the women's anguished cries.

> Throughout the sixties, Beechwood, a large Victorian house in Putney, South-West London, was a conveyor belt of human sadness. (2013)

While John always knew the name of his father, it took a while for him to realize that his father was more than just a 'musician', as recorded in the notes and belongings that Dawn kept. She, as a young model, had been one of the countless young women that Brian had met at The Crawdaddy Club in Richmond-on-Thames in 1965. He was one of the results of the new sexual freedom. He did meet Jones once and was much struck by the resemblance.

Today, according to Scott Jones, John is a senior manager at Ford in Dagenham. He had been put up for adoption but fortunately, he is in close touch with his real mother, as he is with Bill Wyman who is now 87. So gradually

Spotlight: John (Paul Andrew) Molloy

the wall of silence that surrounded his birth was broken down and John even went so far as to visit his grandparents, Lewis and Louisa, in Cheltenham. He should not have been surprised at the outcome.

> I wanted to say hello. These are my grandparents, my flesh and blood. But they refused to acknowledge me. I think it's disgusting how the Jones family has responded to me. I'm not after money – I'm doing all right. This is about who I am. Being acknowledged is a fundamental part of life … To be ignored is an awful thing and that's what the Jones family is doing to me. That really hurts. (2013)

Too much for Cheltenham to put up with.

He learned that Sussex police would not be reopening the case of Brian's death. He finds that unacceptable. Scott Jones wondered what John would do if he had been able to meet Brian latterly.

> First, I'd probably hit him for what he did to Dawn. Then I'd brush him down and ask if he wanted a coffee. I'd like to chat with him. To get to know him and for him to get to know me. He'd like me, I know he would. I'd want him to be proud of me. To be honest, I'd just want him to be my Dad.

But, would Brian have ever been so considerate? It seems rather doubtful.

YOU'D BETTER MOVE ON

For a short while, ensconced in his new Kensington flat with Anita Pallenberg, it seemed as if Brian was finally calming down as he began to enjoy playing host to the then great of the pop world if not the good. This included trans-Atlantic successes such as Bob Dylan and The Byrds. The way the flat was laid out, with its intrinsic style and minstrels' gallery, gave Brian a short period of comfort in that he felt, after a load of grotty digs, this could be a real home for him and Anita. And, for a while, the address became the place to be seen at for the rich and famous. It also had a newly won sense of style. But, as so often with Brian, nothing was really worked for. He was like the child in the sweetshop demanding immediate satisfaction and true inner peace does not come so cheaply.

In the meantime, Andrew Oldham was up to his tricks again and, in an attempt to squeeze Brian out, he used his,

> ... latest technique of only booking interviews with Mick and Keith [which] was keeping Brian out of the headlines. (68, 2016)

This worked so well that the trade papers began asking what had happened to Brian Jones. The one person who did know his whereabouts was Dawn Malloy, the not-so-proud mother of Brian's fifth and final illegitimate child. She was, not unnaturally, seeking a settlement from Jones who adopted his usual stance of ignoring the entire issue. Settlement was eventually left to Oldham who arranged for Brian to pay her a lump sum in return for surrendering all rights and claims to any future income from Jones. She received £700 which does not seem an awful lot even for the time, but she signed the necessary documents and the run of five illegitimate children ceased here as far as we know although some sources cite a sixth or even a seventh example. The matter was then quickly forgotten except, of course, by Dawn.

It was at this point that things began to change significantly with the appointment of the slightly shady cockney, Tom Keylock, an ex-army man,

You'd Better Move On

as chauffeur. However, he was efficient and he soon saw a useful opportunity for himself, as we shall see. According to Pierre Perrone in *The Independent*, Keylock's obituary gave the following information:

> Born in 1926, Keylock joined the Royal Army Service Corps and saw action at the Battle of Arnhem in Holland in 1944. At the end of the Second World War, he was posted to Palestine as Britain surrendered control of the region and the state of Israel declared independence in 1948. After being demobbed, he worked as a driver in and around London. In August 1965, he was hired to take Jagger and Richards to Heathrow airport and did such a great job protecting the Stones stars from fans and photographers that they proposed he come to work for them full-time. Keylock mulled the offer over and finally agreed a month later. (2009)

It was his army training that made him particularly useful to Jagger and Richards when fame eventually came knocking. He was particularly well organized. Originally hired as a chauffeur, when The Stones were mobbed at various venues, Keylock proved an excellent person to have around as a minder. And yet, there is something about pop music success. Despite all the adulation and the money, there was always the stench of something slightly seedy. The industry seems to attract the worst type of people, often ending up in garish headlines in the tabloids. In the case of Tom Keylock it was hard to define until towards the end of Brian's life; it was more a case of continuous suspicion. No matter what happened, he seemed to be there in the background. He was the ultimate minder but somehow there was an indefinable dark side to his influence over the band. He even acted as chauffeur to Bob Dylan on his tour of Britain in May 1966. He had no particular skills other than organization, but he appeared to have a need to be close to the bright lights of celebrities. And it was no doubt useful for The Stones to have Keylock arrange decoy vehicles and alternative routes so that The Stones could arrive and leave crowded venues relatively unimpeded. He was an efficient fixer but violence was often not far away.

Actual violence occurred when on tour with The Stones in Zurich in 1967, Keylock punched a man who invaded the stage to keep him away from the band. Worse, he also got into a fight involving the Greek police in Athens during a concert just days prior to a political coup. This was a man who knew how to defend himself but it was a wonder he was not arrested. As such he was invaluable to The Stones. But his significant claim to fame in this story is for the introduction of Frank Thorogood to The Stones, an undesirable builder who seems inseparable from the tragedy that eventually overtook Brian Jones. He also had, despite being married, a girlfriend, Janet Lawson, who plays a key part as a witness later on. It is for that reason that, despite lack of hard evidence, one eventually comes to question Keylock's motives. He was, after all, the person chosen to look after Brian Jones when he was sacked from the band. If he had been so useful to the band, why did Jagger and Richards choose to sidetrack him unless there was an ulterior motive? There are many unanswered questions concerning him, most significant of which was why did Keylock claim initially that he was not present at Cotchford on the night Brian Jones died and later admit that he was? This may well be the reason he was not interviewed in the allegedly inadequate police enquiry.

Meanwhile, The Stones at this time had developed some connections in high places, as well as low ones, and one of the attractions was Morocco which had come to Brian's attention through Robert Fraser, an old Etonian. The lifestyle there was far more relaxed and exotic than postwar Cheltenham with its pinched and disapproving matrons round every corner who were such anathema to Jones. It also offered opportunities to the other Stones who, having made some cash, were keen to take advantage of the easy-going lifestyle combined with just the right amount of licentiousness. According to Rawlings and Spendel:

> This has much to do with the fact that the Moroccans are not Arabs. They speak Arabic and hold Islam as their official religion but are in fact descended from the Moors, with smatterings from ancient Carthage and Phoenicia, Greece and Rome. With its long established trade links with the rest of Africa, Morocco has developed a culture all of its own; vibrant, strange and dangerous, at least to the impressionable westerner. This was the view held by Brion Gysin, the artist and poet who arrived in Tangier for a short break in 1953 and he was so instantly smitten, he never left. (68/9, 2016)

You'd Better Move On

Of course this was some 10 years before the arrival of Brian Jones but little had changed in the interim and while Gysin was a more conventional poet and artist than Jones, the appeal for both men was similar. There was a very relaxed and often dreamlike atmosphere. After just one trip, Brian felt completely comfortable there and he wandered through the alleys and marketplaces with Anita collecting jewellery and clothing to the manor born, becoming an expert in haggling along the way. But what really appealed to him were the range of strange instruments, some of them completely new to him. It had something of the same appeal that Indian music had for George Harrison of The Beatles – mystical and other worldly. Soon Brian was impressing the locals with his inbuilt ability to play strange instruments with little practice. It was a match made in heaven and a world away from grey old England.

But the downside of this was that drugs were available far more freely than in England and just as he took to the instruments, Brian was keen to try out the drugs, especially as he could do so without either being reported by the neighbours or being answerable to the law. It was a wonderfully relaxed relationship. And beyond that were also the Berber women eager to oblige this import from England. They were totally brazen about it and their very foreignness and tattoos completely appealed to Jones. We know from his past that he was always willing to try something new and this appeared to be a heaven-sent opportunity for Brian to indulge himself without the law looking over his shoulder.

Brian and Anita were staying in the Hotel Minzai in Tangier and they had a wonderful suite overlooking the sea. But none of this was enough for the ungentlemanly Brian who, not for the first time, tried to hit Anita when she disagreed with him but instead he broke his wrist on a wrought-iron windowsill that he had not seen and had to be taken to a clinic to be patched up. Although he felt very sorry for himself, Brian was by this time in deep with a drug dealer and, as a result, the rows with Anita got more frequent and more heated, presumably over money. The end of the relationship was soon on the cards. For the moment though, he arranged for all the stuff they had collected in the markets to be shipped back to England and sold in a newly opened antique shop, although virtually none of it was genuinely antique.

Semi-Detached Suburban Mr Jones

Brian's view was that, since it came from Africa, nobody would question whether an item was genuine or not. This was a pretty naïve approach since, without proper provenance, they would not be bought. In addition, the knowledge of antique experts, as we have seen from the BBC's *Antiques Road Show*, is pretty wide ranging and certainly not confined to the UK. This was just supremely selfish Brian having his own way once again and the base of two candlesticks was stuffed with hash for his use in London. A great way to smuggle it in. So his choice of items to bring back was not in any way confined to the artistic. He also failed to see that his overriding selfishness would not make him happy. Indeed, the more that Brian bought just led to the usual sense of diminishing returns instead of what he perceived would be increased satisfaction. He also totally failed to control his outgoings against his income.

Brian had a ludicrous idea of wealthy whites bringing money and influence to small outlying pockets of Tangier, like Joujouka, so that they could build schools, develop a proper water supply and drainage, and generally develop the community for jobs. It certainly was a very primitive community but for Brian it was just another passing fancy, he never had any intention of putting in the very substantial work needed to achieve it. It also provided a vain hope for the locals which was never realized. Nevertheless, at the time, they were all in some way fascinated by him and that was probably the reason that he began to see himself as The Great Giver. But Brian only looked at things in the short term from what he could get out of it and, of course, no such thing ever happened because Brian had a very short attention span which disappeared along with his apparent magnanimity, but he did make a record of the local music, *Brian Jones presents the Pipes of Pan at Joujouka*, featuring the Master Musicians of Joujouka led by Bachir Attar. This was quite exotic and not to everyone's taste.

With his penchant for drugs, Brian invented a curiosity called The Dream Machine. This had,

> ... two revolving cylinders with holes pierced in them and lights behind them. You looked through the cylinders, the lights made patterns and you were supposed to start dreaming. (70, 2016)

You'd Better Move On

The description raises questions as to whether you would also be absorbing illegal substances while using it. Certainly, the apparent connection between Brian's habit and the nature of the machine cannot be dismissed as entirely coincidental. For some reason he thought it would raise money for the Tangier village and Brian managed to persuade some of his rich friends such as Robert Fraser and Helena Rubinstein to put money into its development. Exactly what happened to that cash we are not sure but in true Jones style, it never got past the development stage and he was very soon on to the next thing.

Meantime Brian's rows with Anita got worse, not helped by an admittance that Marianne Faithfull had slept with him. It ended when Jones hit Anita and chauffeur Keylock took control and told him in no uncertain terms that men don't hit women. It is interesting to compare this with Keylock's attitude towards Frank Thorogood, a schoolfriend who will play a significant part in this story, in far worse circumstances later on. But for Brian there were no boundaries and that relationship (his most prized) went the way of so many others. However, Keylock had begun to show his usefulness to The Stones as a whole and it wasn't long before he became the official road manager in place of Ian Stewart. Keylock, as we know, was extremely efficient at getting The Stones out of trouble when there was a mob outside where they were playing and, being an ex-army man, he also knew how to use his fists if it were necessary.

By 1966 the English capital had become known as 'Swinging London' and The Stones released their first compilation album, *Big Hits, High Tide and Green Grass*. I know this because I bought it and very good it was too, containing many top-flight songs with The Stones at the top of their game. Whether *The Grass* referred to in the title was an oblique reference to drugs I am not sure, but I shouldn't be surprised. It was not that Brian was the only Stone to take drugs, it was just that the others were more canny about it whereas he did it on an industrial scale and it really is amazing that he didn't come to grief considerably earlier than 1969, given his intake of both drugs and booze. At this time LSD and drugs began to be quite widely used and not just by the usual down and outs but also by the rich and famous. The sixties were a time of unprecedented freedom for young people breaking away from the postwar strictures. The Rolling Stones could be seen as influential in setting the pattern for this and while it might, at this distance in time, seem colourful and quaint to us, there is no doubt it had appalling consequences for some families. This was not least due to the increasing availability of drugs and, of course, the money to buy them. Success bred more success with The Stones appearing on television and radio as well as public appearances and outselling The Beatles in terms of records by quite a margin. However, the internal division between Jagger/Richards and Jones got steadily wider.

According to Rawlings and Spendel, and this really is quite surprising:

> Brian boosted his flagging bank account by joining a modelling agency and accepting assignments from trendy fashion designers and magazines. The necessity of becoming the first moonlighting Rolling Stone obviously rankled with him and the gap [between him and the others] widened even further. (71, 2016)

We should question whether it really was such a necessity or simply because Brian could not control himself or his spending. One wonders what such designers and photographers made of the often half-stoned Stone. It seems likely that such photographs would have needed more than a modicum of touching up.

Perhaps the oddest period of all before Brian and Anita split up was when, under her tutelage, he started dressing like she did and wearing her clothes and make-up. The suggestion has been made that she wanted him to look like French singer, the late Françoise Hardy. Being short, Brian seemed to closely resemble her and they often went shopping in the ladies' section of many fashionable stores, buying blouses, hats, scarves and jewellery. As to why Anita encouraged him to do this is not clear but she may have done it to prove that she, being the stronger character, had him completely under her thumb. It also seemed to amuse her. From an outsider's point of view, this cross dressing was not a sign of Brian's hitherto unexplored femininity but just another example of Brian pushing the boundaries of what was acceptable and blurring the divide between male and female. It may also have given Anita a sexual kick. After all, when appearing as The Rolling

Stones they dressed very much in the type of clothes that you could pick up in any high street while this diversion demonstrated a completely different side of Brian's sexuality. It was probably yet another example of Brian rebelling against convention in order to shock. Visiting a respectable hotel in Sherborne not long ago, I was surprised to encounter a husband and wife where he wore high-heeled shoes, make-up and tights topped off by some startling green nail polish. She, normally dressed, didn't seem to mind or even be aware of this transgression. In Brian's case though and despite all attempts to the contrary, his masculinity shone through.

> Small Faces drummer Kenney Jones testified, "He stood out from the others by the way he dressed and which was a million miles away from how we looked: a bunch of Mods. I remember I was shocked when I finally spoke to him. I had expected him to be girlish which was how he looked. What really took me back a step was the fact that he was the very opposite. He had this very deep posh voice and was surprisingly manly. It wasn't how I'd imagined him at all." (73, 2016)

If we look at this behaviour in the light of what was going on in the turbulent sixties, it looks like just another attempt to break down the barriers of conventional behaviour thrown up by the stiff parental regime of the time experienced by Brian and others, all formal cocktail parties and false respect. Brian never seemed to have any respect for anyone except his musical peers and, looking back on his history, he was known for leaving an unholy mess behind him, not to mention at least five broken hearts. In producing at least five illegitimate children by different women who could not see beyond his charisma, he questioned his own legitimacy. He was a broken child who became a broken man.

SPOTLIGHT:
MOROCCO

Morocco offers something a little different from the rest of Africa, a relaxed and friendly environment in a relatively acceptable climate. This had considerable appeal to Brian Jones. The name is an anglicizing of the Spanish *Marruecos*, derived from the city of Marrakesh which was the capital of several local dynasties. The modern Arabic name is *al-Maghreb*, the land of the west or sunset in whose kingdom it is situated. It borders the Mediterranean Sea to the north, the Atlantic to the west, Algeria to the east and the Western Sahara to the west. The current population is close to 40 million and the populace speak Arabic (or a version of it), Berber or English, Spanish and French. However, the Arab influence which has grown since the seventh century is probably strongest. It was ruled by a number of different dynasties and was probably at its peak as a regional power in the 11th and 12th centuries.

In the 15th and 16th century, Morocco faced external threats to its sovereignty, with Portugal seizing some territory and the Ottoman empire encroaching from the east. The Marinid and Saadi dynasties otherwise resisted foreign domination, and Morocco was the only North African nation to escape Ottoman domination ... In 1956, Morocco regained its independence and reunified ... since when it has remained relatively stable. It has the fifth-largest economy in Africa and wields significant influence in both Africa and the Arab world; it is considered to be a middle power in global affairs and holds membership in the Arab League ... Morocco is a unitary semi-constitutional monarchy with an elected parliament. The executive branch is led by the King of Morocco and the prime minister, while legislative power is vested in two chambers of parliament: the House of Representatives and the House of Councillors. Judicial power rests with the Constitutional Court ... The king holds vast executive and legislative powers, especially over the military, foreign policy and religious affairs; he can issue decrees called *dahirs*, which have the force of law, and can also dissolve the parliament after consulting the prime minister and the president of the Constitutional Court. (Wikipedia, 2024)

However, its appeal to Europeans (and Brian Jones) lies in its apparently gentle and exotic atmosphere which draws you in together with its mostly friendly and tolerant population.

COTCHFORD FARM – THE DARK SIDE

When I visited Cotchford Farm in January 2019 it did not strike me as a particularly romantic place, although that may have been partly because it was in the early days of the year and everything was cold and dead. But, leaving that aside, it is not particularly pretty, being stuck at the end of a lane on a site sloping downhill from the road and with many additions made to the property over the centuries. However, it was undoubtedly the building's history and its association with Milne that attracted Jones and, of course, its proximity to Ashdown Forest. It was also not too far from London. While close to the village of Hartfield, its 10 acres offered space and an access to nature that Jones would have found to be a complete contrast to the claustrophobic metropolitan life of an itinerant band member. No stuffy hotel rooms, no cramped vans, no small backstage dressing rooms and, above all, not many people. Furthermore, it took him at the age of 26 a world away from the prissy disapproval of suburban Cheltenham. As we know from previous resident William Young, Cotchford Farm was originally a number of farmers' cottages and before that, in the 16th century, a crown forge. From humble beginnings and an important historical past, it was to see its most dramatic event during the tenancy of Brian Jones, who was already, though he may not have realized it, on a downward path.

The lane on which it is situated is relatively unremarkable and because the land on which the property is situated slopes away, it would be quite hard to appreciate the property fully without entering and understanding the layout and, of course, the swimming pool. It is in effect relatively private and perhaps that is what appealed to Alan Alexander Milne as a suitable country pile. It offered tranquillity in a relatively sylvan setting. It has been altered continuously over the centuries from its early beginnings as a crown forge. It is now quite a mishmash of different styles and although quaint, it could hardly be described as beautiful and the kitchen placed as it is at the bottom of the slope was, in Brian Jones' day, subject to flooding. Terry

Rawlings and Paul Spendel describe it as 'a beautiful Sussex farmhouse' (97, 2016) but I would disagree. You would need to love it because of its age and history to live there and, at the time of my visit, it could scarcely be described as comfortable. Certain rooms are impressive in terms of wood finish while others resemble something of a botch and, in the middle of winter, it seemed rather cold and totally lacking in the magic described by Christopher Robin Milne. But then neither he nor his father seemed particularly worried by lack of comfort as both father and son chose to write in the dingiest and damp of rooms, the father partly at Cotchford and the son in the flat above the bookshop in Dartmouth.

So we may assume that the magical world of Winnie-the-Pooh is largely a creation of the mind and while Ashdown Forest and its literary alternative the Hundred Acre Wood are there for inspection, you cannot really appreciate the charm of the place in the middle of winter. Going back a century or more before the Milnes, Cotchford was a working farm with everything that implies, and it is only relatively recently that it was turned into a country home. With all the differing parts of the building, it cannot be that easy to manage and at the time of visiting, it was proving hard to sell despite its history. The Disney organization wanted it at one point, but they were fortunately resisted. Heaven knows what would have happened to the house if they had gained control. Although, sad to say, presently it is now an Airbnb. So for those who want to know what it was like to grow up in the footsteps of Christopher Robin or even the relatively brief tenure of Brian Jones, the opportunity is there for the taking. However, at the time of writing it will cost you around £1,000 for a brief stay which includes a £100 cleaning charge. Nevertheless, Cotchford does seem to have an indefinable attraction and its history has supplied the material for no less than three books by this writer.

Brian Jones purchased Cotchford Farm on 21st November 1968 for £31,500. It was intended to be a country retreat, a safe haven from the brashness and claustrophobia of the metropolis. It was planned as a place where Brian could become his own person and perhaps bring up children and animals, long after the discordant music of The Rolling Stones had died away. After all, it had served as such for the Milnes and for generations before them, but

Semi-Detached Suburban Mr Jones

the trouble was that Brian was not his own man. In his saner moments, and these were becoming precious few, Brian wanted to resume the comfortable middle-class life from which he had sprung even if his parents refused to let him enjoy it in Cheltenham. But the dominant strain of Brian's life was still music, something that seemed out of kilter with the East Sussex farmhouse and its environs.

Geoffrcy Giuliano describes Cotchford Farm as a place for,

> … the grown up Christopher Robin of the Woodstock generation to seek refuge from the unremitting pressures and adulation that made and then unmade The Stones' golden haired guitarist. (86, 1994)

At this point in his account of Brian Jones' life, *Paint It Black*, Giuliano makes some assertions about the Milnes which are just plain incorrect and, because of that, one worries about the accuracy of other parts of the book. He suggests that:

> After Milne died in 1956, the old man's famous son put the premises up for sale, ultimately assuming an anonymous life in Brighton as an antiques dealer. (86, 1994)

Nothing could be further from the truth since the property passed to A. A. Milne's wife, Daphne. Also Christopher Milne's postwar career was spent running a successful bookshop in Dartmouth for 21 years with his wife. In addition, the farm was sold on Daphne's death after she had deliberately destroyed A. A. Milne's possessions. There is a strange echo of this in Keylock's destruction of some of Jones' things soon after his death, possibly at the behest of his father, Lewis.

Mary Hallett was housekeeper to the Milnes at Cotchford for many years. Sadly she lost both her first husband to meningitis and her son who was run over and killed not far from the farm. She also remains the only stable influence in this story. With these tragedies in mind, she was delighted to make the acquaintance of Brian Jones when he bought the house from the previous owners, the Taylors. Their only relevance to this story is that they were the ones who put in the swimming pool in the rear garden, and, in so doing, set the scene for the tragedy to come.

Dick Hattrell had this to say about his final visit to Cotchford:

> Brian also restored all the little stone statues around the pool Milne had fashioned after the characters in his book. Brian loved the house because *Winnie-the-Pooh* had been one of his favourite books and he used to read passages from it out loud. (112, 1994)

Initially Brian Jones' life at Cotchford seemed everything he hoped it would be. According to Giuliano:

> For the first time in years he'd found the presence of mind to be alone and think deeply. Suddenly there was no pressure to perform, or indeed do anything at all. Like the dreamy Christopher Robin walking the dew covered fields of Pooh Corner, Jones spent days wandering the self-same spaces as the former master of the house. (85, 1994)

This sounds very romantic except of course that Christopher Robin was never the master of Cotchford Farm. Just the son, growing up. When Alan Milne died, the property passed to his wife, Daphne, not Christopher Robin. On purchasing Cotchford, Brian Jones then made a comment to a journalist which seems strangely prescient.

> This place is me, man … I'll never leave here I'm sure. (85, 1994)

And, of course, he never did, except in death. It seems particularly sad that Cotchford, where Brian Jones initially felt most at ease, was to be the scene of his ultimate destruction.

Mary Hallett recalls seeing the young Christopher Robin happily playing in the garden and now here was someone who seemed to appreciate what Cotchford stood for. When Milne died in 1956, the property was put up for sale and it was then bought by a wealthy young couple, the Taylors. Stewart Taylor was an American and his wife, Margarita, was Spanish. Mary Hallett initially offered to clean for them. They were so pleased with her work that when the couple eventually split up in 1967 and the house was once again on the market, the Taylors insisted that part of the deal was that Mary be kept on as housekeeper. As it happens, she was used to celebrities, since actor Richard Harris had rented the property from the Taylors at one point

Semi-Detached Suburban Mr Jones

while they were abroad. So while Mary was wondering about the nature of her new employer, there had been radio silence as to just who it might be.

According to Geoffrey Giuliano, this was how Mary Hallett remembered meeting Brian:

> The first time I actually saw Brian was when he came to meet the Taylors. He was walking down the drive and I was going up … He was dressed in a fur coat and shoulder-length hair. I thought it was a woman! He was very nice when I spoke to him. He looked rather like Pooh Bear coming home again. (87, 1994)

Yet Giuliano then contradicts himself. He wanted to become part of the Cotchford Farm set but somehow he could not fit in. He was, according to Giuliano:

> Well known for his outrageous, gender-bending costumes, eye make-up and effeminate manner. By the time he moved to Cotchford he consciously rejected all that in favour of a more confident, less dramatic, conservative look. (90, 1994)

Michael Martin, the gardener, who had also been included in the package, remembers that winter day when,

> … this Rolls Royce pulled into the drive. It had tinted windows so we still couldn't see who was in it. Then this dolly-bird got out and minced up the path and introduced herself as a secretary and told us we were now working for The Rolling Stones. (98, 2016)

Initially, neither Michael nor Mary wanted to work for such a group, being well aware of their reputation. Matters were not helped when a man in a fur cape and a woman's hat emerged from the car and strode right past the gardener without so much as a word. When Mary's daughter, Linda, first spotted him she thought Jones was a woman because of course he was still going through the previously mentioned cross-dressing stage. So his arrival did nothing to dispel Mary and Michael's concern and an initial decision to leave.

But too much water had already gone under the bridge and the die was already cast. Her description was fanciful but there is no doubt that, of all his contacts at Cotchford, Mary Hallett got the best of him. Brian was playing a role in a life where he was only partly in control and, as he did so, with the money, the drink and the drugs, there were vultures gathering with the sole aim of getting their share of the action. So the Cotchford Farm portrayed in this story took on a very different atmosphere from my previous subjects. Cut off from the community, after Brian's arrival, it ceased to be a sanctuary and became the stage for the undesirable nature that Brian seemed to carry with him.

Amazingly, Brian's tenure of Cotchford was little more than seven months and while much has been written about what happened there on that night of 2nd July 1969, it is a mere blip in the long and continuing history of this 16th-century farmhouse. We should also remember that when he bought Cotchford he was still a Rolling Stone but when he died, just a few short months later, he was not. In the space of just 27 short years, his ambition as well as his life had been terminated. The curious thing is that despite its apparent peace and tranquillity, Jones always seemed to attract there the very things that he alleged he was trying to get away from. The best thing about it was undoubtedly Mary Hallett who had lived locally all her life and, in 1967, was acting housekeeper to the property. However, despite her innate goodness and stability she was quite unable to stop the train of events there from taking place. She took to Brian straight away and he seems to have reserved his best side for her. As a result, he found a good friend in her while she regarded him, with his short stature and blond mop, as some kind of substitute for her lost son. Mary Hallett had, in her long life, seen the transformation of a one-time working farm together with its labourers' cottages and other outbuildings, into a stylish retreat for upmarket clients with the lifestyle to go with it. You only need to go back to its situation to the 1850s to understand the enormous changes that have taken place there. My earlier book, *The Diary of William Young of Cotchford Farm* (2022), gives a clear idea of just how different that was and how in the space of about a century, it had become a desirable country residence for the Milnes. The work needed to transform the house was largely overseen by Milne's extremely capable wife Daphne (née de Sélincourt).

However, things were to radically change when Mary finally met Brian Jones.

He was the most polite and kindest boy I've ever known. You could not have wished for a nicer boy. He was kindness itself. (99, 2016)

According to Giuliano, Mary tells us:

We used to talk a lot. We often discussed the Bible. He said he thought that living on e[E]arth was the hell and that heaven would come after. At times I think he was very unhappy. Fame and money didn't really bring him any good things. He certainly wasn't crazy as people often say, he was a lovely boy. (88, 1994)

Perhaps the most surprising story about Brian came from Michael Martin, who was a lay preacher at the local church. He tells us that Brian knew the Bible inside out and often read and quoted from it. This seems surprising given his history. This is the man who was prepared to steal from his friends and colleagues and leave the mothers of his illegitimate children in the lurch. It was as if Brian knew what he ought to be doing but was too weak minded ever to achieve it.

The following is a simple example. Despite their friendship, Brian, ever the prankster, still could not resist playing a trick on Mary Hallett. Brian asked her to have a drink with him but she explained that she was virtually a non-drinker. So he said he would not give her more than a quarter of a glass and he kept to his word, except for the fact that the glass he used was a pint one, leaving Mary to get unusually squiffy on spirits, much to Brian's delight, and have trouble making her way home. Somewhat unkind to a woman who he could rely on and who treated him so well.

At Cotchford he seemed a world away from the wild child we have heard about earlier. Perhaps he really did intend to settle down in the East Sussex countryside and re-establish his middle-class credentials. Whatever his motives, Mary Hallett, reliable and completely unthreatening, became perhaps Brian's only true friend at Cotchford but, sadly, she also became a witness when, in the following months, things took a turn for the worse. Michael Martin also eventually accepted his new employer, especially when Brian sometimes worked alongside him in the garden. It seemed like an idyllic arrangement and perhaps it would have been, had not all the things that Brian was trying to escape from in London started to intrude on life at Cotchford. He simply was not a strong enough character to completely reject them.

It may have seemed as if Brian's sojourn at Cotchford would be a new start in the company of his latest girlfriend, model Suki Potier. They appeared to be cut from the same cloth and she certainly had an element of wildness about her. He had met her at the Guinness ancestral home in Ireland in 1966, but they did not become close until about a year later. Because of his background, it was probably easier for Brian to mix with the upmarket set than other members of the group. Just how close he got to Suki is a matter for speculation because Brian still hankered after Anita Pallenberg, whose strong charisma and sexuality had never, in his view, been bettered in anyone else. While trivial in many of her pursuits, Suki's connection with Brian was often more of a mother protector than a girlfriend.

> 'I loved him deeply,' she confided in a rare interview shortly after Brian's death … 'He could be a right bastard at times, lashing out at the people who loved him, but all that was only on the surface.' (89, 1994)

She realized that his parental problems were at the root of the trouble, but one questions whether that could entirely justify his behaviour.

> 'All he ever wanted was the simple love and comfort of a home and family, but like an old dog, he had been kicked so long and so hard all that was buried underneath years of hurt and resentment.'

> Brian was close to Suki, but not particularly affectionate, or ever really committed. 'Believe me, *Brian* was the only woman he ever really loved,' said Suki in a telling remark. (89, 2016)

At the end of the day, she was just not Anita Pallenberg.

Jones was certainly steeped in his own selfishness. On one occasion Brian's friend, Christopher Gibbs, a Chelsea antiques dealer, reports that while Brian and Suki were on holiday in Marrakesh, he received a panic-stricken call from Brian so he rushed to their suite.

> The bed [was] covered, like everything else in shards of jagged glass. Unconscious, Suki was badly bruised and bleeding from a deep gash on her forehead. (92, 2016)

Semi-Detached Suburban Mr Jones

It took some time for Gibbs to persuade Brian to call a doctor. So she put up with an awful lot from him and he did not deserve her. The following day it was as if nothing had ever happened and the two of them carried on with their spending spree. Whatever he did, Suki seemed to be able to forgive him. Heaven knows why she stayed with him for as long as she did.

With regard to the massive amount of items he collected, one wonders whether this was simply a reaction against the recent past with The Stones or whether it demonstrated his middle-class values. There was a William Morris [of Arts and Crafts fame] tapestry, a large Edwardian woven screen. There were also a number of Moroccan items, resulting from trips to the markets in Marrakesh and Tangier. Gibbs reports that:

> Brian and I used to swan around the local cafes and markets smoking joints and generally enjoying ourselves. The problem was that Brian was always so supremely paranoid he was convinced that people were out get him. (92, 1994)

While that paranoia was initially misplaced, by the time he got to Cotchford, Jones' worries started to become rooted in reality.

Suki Potier's life was, incidentally, sadly cut short when she died in a car accident in Portugal on June 25th 1981. She was just 34. She deserved better than that and better than Brian who totally failed to reward her loyalty. As Giuliano points out:

> The truth is, Brian was far too concerned with getting himself straight, mentally and physically, to have an awful lot of himself left over to give to anyone. 'Someday ...' Potier remembers him saying softly, 'Someday, I'll be better and it won't have to be this way anymore.' So Suki waited – just like poor Pat Andrews, Linda Lawrence, Linda Keith and the other young willing women whose names history fails to record. And, of course, sadly, 'someday' never came. (90, 1994)

After settling in to Cotchford, Brian decided on another holiday. Visiting Sri Lanka, or Ceylon as it was then, Brian and Suki Potier met the science fiction writer, Arthur C. Clarke, who originated the concept of the communications satellite. According to Giuliano the *elderly* (my italics) Clarke

1 335, Hatherley Road, Cheltenham, where Brian Jones grew up.

2 Cotchford Farm and its swimming pool.

3 Tom Keylock. Stones' roadie and eventually Brian Jones' minder.

4 Frank Thorogood comforts Brian Jones' girlfriend Anna Wohlin as they arrive at Brian's inquest.

5 Frank Thorogood in old age. How are the mighty fallen!

6 Louisa, Lewis and Barbara Jones at the funeral. Behind is Frank Thorogood.

7 Brian Jones' coffin entering St Mary's Parish Church, Cheltenham.

8 Brian Jones' grave in Cheltenham Cemetery 3 July 2019, the 50th anniversary of his death.

9 Brian Jones' grave in 2024 showing recent gifts.

took him to meet a man who claimed to have been Hitler's personal astrologer. Jones was told 'not to go swimming without a friend. The water holds much danger for you.' Not unnaturally, Brian failed to take him seriously and laughed. But the man persisted and finished with a final warning: to beware of false friends. I am somewhat dubious about this whole story because, at the time of their visit, Clarke would have been about 50, not in the least elderly since he was born in 1917. The whole thing smacks somewhat of a gypsy fortune teller with a crystal ball. Clarke emigrated to Sri Lanka to follow his interest of scuba diving, also finding hidden temples underneath the sea. He also fronted a couple of television series. But why would such a learned man have any interest in the effete and essentially shallow Brian Jones? It is hard to decide except for the fact that there would have been relatively few other English on the island at any one time.

On returning, Brian realized belatedly that Cotchford needed substantial renovations. For a number of reasons it might have been wiser to have done that before purchasing all these items. As a result, he felt he needed to employ a builder to bring the place up to standard.

> The old farmhouse needed much more than new curtains and furnishings and so [Brian] got in touch with The Stones' office in Maddox Street in London, requesting help in organising some serious interior decorations. (92, 1994)

If only that had come to fruition. When Brian Jones first arrived at Cotchford he wanted to make a splash in a different way to his past. He wanted to turn it into a desirable country residence, to turn heads by converting this rather ramshackle building into something remarkable.

> Brian sought to decorate his prize with the finest furnishings his often sporadic income might allow. He and Suki searched the antique markets off the King's Road for pieces that would distinguish Cotchford, and its owner, as being at the very pinnacle of good taste and refinement. (91, 1994)

It is a pity that they didn't come up with any names because Tom Keylock came to the fore, suggesting an old school friend of his, Frank Thorogood, who had previously done some work for Keith Richards; not very satisfactorily it has to be said.

> Among the many stories relating to Thorogood was a charge made by Keith that several people in Thorogood's employ were steadily and gleefully ripping him off. When Thorogood went to work for Brian, Richards warned the errant builder about attempting any liberties with his new employer. (93, 1994)

To no avail. This begs the question as to why use him again. Why not get somebody more professional? Keith was nevertheless,

> ... assured that Brian would be well looked after. 'That's what I'm afraid of,' Richards reportedly replied. (93, 1994)

Francis Thorogood appears to have been an East End hard man and cheap crook known for cutting corners who was not a skilled builder and for whom no botch and no overcharge was too much trouble. He was also a petty thief, a quality that he shared with Brian. Quite why Brian did not consider some more suitable candidates before alighting on Thorogood is not clear, but it was probably lack of experience. Thorogood had also worked for photographer David Bailey and neither Richards nor Bailey had been satisfied with the results. This makes the decision even more inexplicable, except for his connection with his schoolfriend, Keylock, on whom the jury is still out.

So the hitherto peaceful community of Cotchford Farm became a tinder box, and Brian Jones,

> ... a prime target for the full gambit of fraud, theft and deception the shifty Thorogood carried round in his hip-pocket. "Like lambs to the slaughter," one Stones intimate later remembered. "Frank had Brian marked as easy pickings from the day he moved in." (93, 1994)

Thorogood, seeing his opportunity, put in a suspiciously round figure estimate of £10,000 for the work which Brian had requested. The former said the work would only be prolonged if he had to travel back and forth to his home in London so it was agreed that the small flat above the garage block, previously used for storage, could be converted and Mary Hallett began to move the contents elsewhere so that Thorogood could move in. This should have been a red warning light to Jones. How many builders actually want to live on the premises? But it was only the beginning. The flat gave Thorogood the chance to move in with his mistress, Joan Fitzsimons, even though he still kept a wife at his London address. In addition, a couple of Frank's so-called assistants moved in as well, Mo and Johnny with their associated women. These two were no better than Frank and soon Cotchford began to take on a rather seedy air with any building work becoming a distant second to these three reprobates enjoying themselves. The effect on Cotchford was disastrous and it soon began to resemble a builder's yard.

Since Brian was completely unskilled in building work or indeed what it should cost, he had agreed to it without any understanding of proper costing or, worse still, the consequences. Tom Keylock, previously of some assistance to The Stones, was entirely responsible for setting up this arrangement and it was he who agreed to supervise the work. Only he didn't and things began to deteriorate very quickly. Brian, it has to be said, did not approve of this arrangement but he seemed unable to do anything about it. He did not want it known that Cotchford, in respectable Hartfield, had effectively become a brothel at the hands of these men. Yet he was completely unable to confront them about it. It was at this point that the balance of power began to imperceptibly shift away from Brian Jones just as it was doing with The Stones. He completely lacked the strength of character or consistency of thought to deal with it.

> Thorogood's long association with Keylock meant that the builder
> was given trustee status. He was therefore awarded special
> privileges. (100, 2016)

These privileges amounted to Thorogood doing more or less exactly what he liked with very little work done, and what work was achieved was of very poor quality. Worse still, Keylock managed to arrange with The Stones' office in London that Thorogood, in addition to the quoted sum, should receive day-to-day living expenses. These would eventually be charged back to Brian, a decision he had absolutely no say in whatsoever. At this point we might question what motive the previously efficient Keylock had in making these arrangements, especially given Thorogood's reputation which he must have been well aware of. Keylock seemed to be completely

Semi-Detached Suburban Mr Jones

in his thrall. Was he deliberately trying to cause harm to the weak-minded Jones or get back at him for some imagined sleight, or getting a substantial kickback? But worse still, incredibly, Keylock, who was still doing occasional work for the other Stones, seems to have handed Thorogood the position of Brian's unofficial minder and Thorogood, a hard East Ender, was determined to take full advantage of it. Yet I have doubts about this report since Thorogood's time at Cotchford was inevitably limited even before what happened on 2nd July 1969, so it seemed to have little point.

Brian and Suki had enjoyed had their holiday in Marrakesh immensely and Brian seemed more relaxed than he had been for some time. But the problems started immediately they got home and life began to take on similarities to the prophecy he was warned about in Sri Lanka. Thorogood was a complete bastard, greedy and manipulative. Returning to Cotchford, they were greeted by the alarming state of the kitchen, empty wine bottles everywhere and dirty dishes in the sink. Clearly no work had been done. A fence that should have been erected in Jones' absence lay untended exactly where it had been when they left previously and yet he was paying Thorogood substantial money. In the end Brian got a friend from the village to erect it instead. More seriously, there was also reputedly a large amount of money hidden, none too well, round the house, perhaps as much as £75,000 and some Swiss francs. Yet this quietly and systematically disappeared. Of course, one can blame Jones for not putting it somewhere safe but it should never have been taken. And this was just the beginning. Brian took the loss with a certain amount of *sangfroid* but did absolutely nothing about improving security.

> "Gone. Ripped off." Gardener Michael Martin confirmed ... that large amounts of cash went missing during Thorogood's reign at Cotchford ... "By his [Jones'] bed there were always piles of money, just lying there ... When the police searched the house they couldn't find a single note. Not one." (96, 1994)

These incidents demonstrate just how weak Brian Jones was; that rather than immediately sacking Thorogood he continued to put up with him despite no proper work being achieved. It also explains how he gradually became taken over by this evil individual. And yet Jones, suffering from paranoia, had always felt, wherever he was, that there were people out to get him, unseen, ubiquitous, but ever present. When incidents such as the missing money occurred it simply confirmed his worse fears. He was just totally unable to do anything about it. He often cried for assistance but by now his friends and colleagues were only too aware of Brian's failings and were mostly fed up with having to bail him out. This reached such a pitch that many avoided his telephone calls, immediately sensing trouble. All of this of course simply played into Thorogood's hands. So Jones was often left entirely alone and the rustic charm of Cotchford began to morph into a nightmare.

Another problem seemed to come from inside Jones himself. He craved attention but at the same time was convinced that those around him were seeking to rob him or destroy him. Frank Thorogood milked it for all was it worth, attempting to undermine him and to make Jones wonder if he was going insane.

A friend described,

> ... "the terrible tricks played by Frank." Brian went to a cupboard for a glass and found a large dead cat lying there as stiff as a board. (115, 1994)

This of course was no accident but one of a series of jolts inflicted on the unfortunate Jones, such as interrupting his telephone calls by disconnecting the line. It was cruel and it bore some relation to such psychological horror films as Hammer's *Taste of Fear* (Columbia, 1961, d. Seth Holt). But worse was to come.

The other big problem for Brian was The Rolling Stones themselves. Known initially for their personal appearances rather than their record sales, Brian had gradually metamorphosed from founder and leader into the lame duck of the group. Surprisingly popular with the female fans to the annoyance of Mick Jagger, the latter began to look for ways to dispose of him. That he was unable to go the States because of drug convictions was one useful lever. Despite his inherent ability with instruments, his poor health often meant that Jones was often unavailable to perform. This together with his total insecurity gave Jagger what he needed to cut him out and replace him with

Semi-Detached Suburban Mr Jones

someone more dedicated. He was fed up with supporting Jones, however potentially talented. So there was now a two-pronged attack forming on Brian. Unbeknownst to Jagger, he was also helping set the scene for the final act in the tragedy. According to Giuliano:

> Stone's [Stones'!] intimate, Ronni Money, wife of eccentric
> performer Zoot Money, knew Brian and the situation very well.
> "Mick was relentless in his pressure to get Jones out of the band …
> He played on all of Brian's weaknesses, his paranoiac insecurity, his
> alcohol dependency, his fears and his self-destructive impulses." (97,
> 1994)

In the meantime, Frank Thorogood, aware how Jones' position had begun to slip with The Stones,

> … systematically turned up the heat at home. He saw to it that
> Brian's life was made as consistently uncomfortable as possible.
> Whether it was hiding his motorbike in the shrubbery, jumping up
> to intercept his phone calls, mercilessly ordering him about or even
> shadowing him, Thorogood's petty campaign of terror kept Jones so
> on edge … that he eventually caved in and hid inside the bottle. (102,
> 1994)

We are not told what part Tom Keylock played in all this but presumably it suited his purpose as well. After all, he was the one that nominated Thorogood.

Brian had decked out Cotchford in all manner of different things including a whole range of largely inappropriate so-called antiques, rugs and screens from Tangier. The house was being decorated in a style befitting a Rolling Stone posing as a country gentleman rather than the genuine article. In addition, Giuliano tells us that:

> One of the first things they bought was an obscenely expensive
> William Morris tapestry of the Elfin King, cavorting with his wee
> subjects in the wood. Another was a large Edwardian woven screen
> of a long-haired little boy sitting pensively in a garden gazing at
> his reflection in a deep pool. Brian used to think it looked rather
> like him. Today it is leaning against a wall in the newspaper strewn

parlour at Mary Hallett's. Lewis Jones gave it to her after Brian died. Another prize is an intricately carved, teak inlaid Moroccan end-table, presented to her by Brian himself, which she proudly shows off to each and every visitor. (91, 1994)

Mary was, despite everything, somehow proud of Brian and she had developed a very close relationship with him in the seven short months he lived at Cotchford. She, deep in her heart, felt that, with Brian, there was an inner loneliness and lack of peace.

Mary Hallett was also somewhat suspicious of Suki and thought that she may have been out for what she could get. So, recognizing the position, Suki may have sided with the stronger man, Thorogood, unconsciously aiding and abetting him. On the other hand, it may not have been that calculated, just the efforts of a frustrated woman to get certain matters sorted out. She certainly seemed to love Jones. If that was the case, she may have been quite unaware just how unscrupulous Thorogood would be with whatever she told him. The problem with Brian was that he did not have enough personality to control events, and he was utterly unreliable. One may think that being in a successful rock band is not a credible way to live but the fact is, in order to retain that success, it takes an enormous amount of organization. And Brian Jones was simply not organized in the way that the other band members were. He was a liability. He was effectively a child behaving badly, operating in a fantasy world without any moral anchor nor awareness of the consequences of his actions. He may have impressed some, but he was ultimately an empty vessel adrift among ill-chosen and far more determined companions.

The decorations gave the farm a slightly exotic and non-English feel as Brian did not care a hoot about the farm's long history except in respect of Winnie-the-Pooh, even though Rawlings alleges that William the Conqueror once stayed there. (99, 2016) The Pooh stories were drawn from two of Brian's favourite books and it seems likely that the idyllic childhood depicted in it was what he might have wistfully wished for himself in Cheltenham, had there not been the continuing stand-off between him and his parents almost from the get go. But then again it was not always idyllic for the real Christopher Robin either because he felt his father had harnessed

Semi-Detached Suburban Mr Jones

his good name for profit when he was too young to do anything about it. According to Rawlings and Spendel, Brian,

> … liked nothing better than to drag guests excitedly around the grounds to show off the pool and the life-size statue of Christopher Robin, leaving until last the sundial which he would point to and then read aloud the inscription: 'This warm and happy spot belongs to Pooh, and here he wonders what to do.' (99, 2016)

Perhaps we all search for an elusive happiness in this life but for Brian, Cotchford seemed to offer the opportunity to catch up on a lost childhood. However, it is alleged that in his darker moods he wanted to take a sledge-hammer to the sundial, echoing his behaviour with childhood toys. It was really only Mary Hallett and perhaps Michael Martin for whom he reserved the hidden good side of his character. What Cotchford offered was a certain peace for those who wished to draw on it, but Brian lacked the stability to take full advantage. His life so far had been an unholy mix of ambition and talent circumscribed by an overwhelming lack of consideration for the needs of others. It was a wholly indigestible mix for such an undisciplined individual who spent the not inconsiderable money he made faster than it was coming in. So while The Stones were becoming unbelievably success-ful, Brian Jones was travelling in the opposite direction.

Initially, there was no doubt that the country air at Cotchford did Brian a power of good and he began to reinterest himself in his music and took pleasure in playing for anyone who would listen. Mary Hallett had to con-stantly remind him that there were close neighbours and he shouldn't make too much noise, but while Brian was initially anxious to keep on good terms with the locals, he didn't always consider them properly in this respect. Giuliano tells us that:

> It is important to remember that Brian, so long deliberately out to shock and cause distress, now wanted nothing more than to become part of the close-knit rural community he called home. … Brian knew well the simple, unaffected people he was dealing with and went out of his way not to antagonise them or cause offence. (90, 2016)

Cotchford Farm – The Dark Side

However, I don't entirely agree with this statement. There is no evidence that Brian was effeminate whilst wearing female clothing as that claim had been discounted by several sources. Rather the reverse with his masculinity showing through all the time, according to the evidence. Also, I take issue that the East Sussex people with whom he mixed at Cotchford were either 'simple' or necessarily 'unaffected'. Certainly he may have thought it best to try and fit in but Brian, being Brian, was usually unable to achieve it except on relatively rare occasions. What he had needed right from the start, as with his parents, was the support of others but he was often quite unaware of the best way to go about it and totally failed to see how his behaviour alienated people.

If Brian was keen to make Cotchford a spectacularly attractive property and did his best to achieve that, the builders didn't help. It was just that, despite being a paid member of The Stones, the money just did not come in fast enough for him to spend it and he was often short. He had no clue about financial management. Everything, even at his level, was just hand to mouth. It would have been far better if he had employed accountants to look after his finances. They could have made him wealthy. Instead, all income was now being filtered through the management company who, not unreasonably, took their share. He wanted to be seen as a man of excellent taste and refinement, the very essence of a country gentleman. But, alas, he wasn't. He was merely playing at it. It was soon after this that things took a turn for the worse.

It is all the more ironic that, about this time and just before the arrival of Thorogood, Rawlings and Spendel provide the following picture of Brian at Cotchford:

> 'These are real people,' … going on to describe his new country neighbours as 'down to earth folk just going about their business, doing real jobs, not like those bastards and junkies [!] up in London.' He found it hard to believe just how removed he had become from enjoying the simple pleasures of life.

> Brian was clearly enjoying his role as country squire and villager, going for long walks down the lanes and across the fields, with his

dog chasing wildly behind him. He was looking fitter than he had for a long time, and friends who visited Brian at Cotchford were amazed at the change in him. (101, 2016)

However, Brian must have realized that his position in The Rolling Stones was problematic, partly due to his own eccentric making and the fact that the police on both sides of the Atlantic were toughening up on drug taking. Brian had already been arrested for possession of drugs two years earlier in May 1967. Amongst the many substances found in his flat were cocaine, marijuana and methamphetamine. While he confessed to the use of marijuana, he said he did not use hard drugs. Giuliano had been wrong about Christopher Robin being of 'the Woodstock generation', but Brian Jones certainly was. Whether this habit accelerated his by now fairly violent mood swings we cannot be sure, but certainly he could change from being friendly and caring to being vicious and problematic in an instant. This, of course, often meant that he could be hell to live with both personally and professionally.

Yet, in May 1968 he was rearrested while he was still on probation from the first bust. This time it was serious; he could be facing jail. Amazingly, the judge was sympathetic and, surprisingly, merely fined him £50 plus £105 in costs. This doesn't sound much now but it was equivalent to at least 10 times as much today. These arrests combined with his other medical problems meant that he was not in a fit condition to tour in this country, let alone abroad. On the occasions he did appear his bandmates would often turn off his amplifier, so little confidence did they have in him. By early 1969, looking frail and uncertain, it was clear Brian had become a liability.

For a while Brian seemed to enjoy his new life at Cotchford. But, after holidaying in Ceylon with Suki:

They returned to England on 12th January [1969] in order for Brian's appeal [against drug conviction] to be heard in court. It was denied, leaving Brian with two convictions to his credit. Suki felt that Brian knew then [five months before he was finally sacked] that he was finally finished as a Rolling Stone. They [the other members of the band] had long since stopped inviting or even informing him of sessions. (102, 2016)

This turned Brian back towards his old habits of booze and drugs, stumbling from one unnecessary party to another, from one club to another in London, in the company of the very hangers-on and junkies he had only recently condemned at Cotchford. He was now an alcoholic. This was the beginning of the end and Suki watched his gradual slide down the slippery slope to oblivion with concern. When he did return to Cotchford, his attitude had changed and the locals, who had originally taken him to their hearts now found that he was a bad-tempered, drunken and inconsiderate oaf who seemed no longer to care about his position there or about what the neighbours thought. Some of them wished him gone and he soon was, but not in the way they had thought. In addition to the drinking there was increasingly wild behaviour locally which included,

> ... crashing his scooter through the window of the shop opposite [The Hay Wagon Inn]. (102, 2016)

From being relatively toned when he first arrived at Cotchford, Brian became overweight and bloated with bags under his eyes, a beard and the blond mop, previously his pride and joy, became dirty, uncut and unkempt. He suffered from violent mood swings from wild exhilaration to deep depression and Suki realized it was time for her to leave. There was simply nothing she could do to control him. Explaining her reasons to Brian, in his usual style he seemed not to have cared less, and though she eventually tried to return, he was never close enough to her for this show of defiance to have had any effect. She still loved him but the strain of trying to live with him was intolerable. He was, as so many had found out before her, quite impossible.

Gardener Martin, realizing what was happening to Brian, desperately tried to get him to take a holiday but Brian kept prevaricating.

> With the stability that Suki offered now gone, Brian's interest in the day-to-day running of Cotchford all but vanished. His accusations concerning Frank and Suki had hardly improved the already shaky situation with the builder, he now avoided even the smallest confrontation. (102, 2016)

Thorogood, on the other hand, easily recognized the inherent weakness of his so-called boss and began to sink his claws in even deeper, taking more and more advantage. His interest in the building work was superficial and second only to an innate sadism. He then casually informed Brian that the poky flat above the garage was inadequate for his purposes and he wanted something more comfortable. So he had decided that the best thing for him and his men was to move into the house. Brian, incredibly stupidly, did not raise a murmur and we can draw a comparison between his shaky situation in The Rolling Stones with the weak position he had been reduced to at his own property. It was extraordinary how fast this happened and how Brian, the once cruel prankster and musician that everyone looked up to had quickly become the victim in what was fast becoming a very dangerous game. We can only guess at exactly what Tom Keylock's motives were in all this. What we do know is that Brian weakly complained to his friends that the builders were not doing their job. Instead, and to the horror of Mary Hallett, they were living the high life on whatever they could find at Cotchford. This included taking food and booze, of which there was a plentiful supply. It was literally open house for the unpleasant Thorogood and his men.

Yet Brian took absolutely no action against these transgressions and continued to deteriorate during a series of parties where all the most disreputable elements that he had said previously he wished to rid himself of were present. Many of these came from London and Cotchford began to get a very undesirable reputation with the neighbours who had once been prepared to welcome him. I want to emphasize just how things had changed in such a very short space of time and that the ensuing tragedy seemed quite unstoppable. However much one regarded Brian Jones as a relatively worthless character, it is difficult not to feel shocked at the turn things were now taking. Far from being Brian's minder, Thorogood was becoming his nemesis and he lost no chance to discomfort him.

To be fair to the other Stones, they realized that Brian was becoming very sick and on a downward path, and despite their differences, they did try to do something about it. They contacted Alexis Korner who you will recall gave Brian his first big break, asked for his advice and he, without promising any results, agreed to visit Brian as if it was a normal social call. Rawlings and Spendel explain that:

Cotchford Farm – The Dark Side

> Korner decided to take his wife Bobbie and young daughter Sappho [!] down to Cotchford. He hadn't seen Brian for some time and was looking forward to meeting up with his old friend. When he arrived at the house, Korner was greatly shocked by Brian's appearance. "He looked like a fat mummified Louis the Fourteenth." ... For his part, Brian was pleased to see the Korners and the group sat and talked for hours about his future plans. (103, 2016)

Korner noted that Brian was drinking heavily and that, amazingly, he sometimes fell asleep in mid-sentence. Eventually, Brian got round to revealing the antagonism between himself and the builders.

> He was keen to point out the parts of the house that, supposedly, had been either refurbished or renovated. He would point to this part or that saying: 'That cost me such and such.' Korner noticed that these particular parts of the house were half-finished or not touched at all. (103, 2016)

It was then obvious to Korner that that the builders were cowboys. He then left saying that he expected to return in a few days and that he would telephone to make a new arrangement. When he did so as promised,

> ... he was disturbed to hear Brian speaking almost in a whisper and pleading for Alexis to visit. "Brian was saying that since my last visit someone had been locking him in the house." (103, 2016)

Initially, both Korner and Mrs Hallett had thought that Brian had mislaid the keys while under the influence but it soon became clear that something more sinister was going on and that this was just one of a series of increasingly nasty tricks perpetrated by Thorogood with the object of wearing Brian down and, possibly, sending him over the edge.

> Alexis told Brian not to panic and said he would be down soon. He assumed that Brian was mislaying the keys himself. Mrs Hallett thought the same at first when Brian would turn up on her doorstep. "We would go out shopping and when we came back he would be sitting there waiting for us. He would be lost because there was no-one in the house to let him in." (103, 2016)

Thorogood was, none too subtly, taking over. It seems like the plot of a 'B' movie, yet it was actually happening.

When Korner finally revisited, he found Brian's mood had lifted and he was altogether sunnier and they discussed going on the road with Korner's band, The New Church. While Brian was really keen to do this because it would get him away from Cotchford, Korner, very sensibly, had to refuse him since, in Brian's present state, he would become a liability rather than an asset, just as he already was with The Stones. He put this to Brian as gently as he could because he did not want to upset Brian's already fragile ego so he leavened it with the suggestion that he would help Brian form a new band by suggesting a list of players and setting a target of six months to bring it to fruition. The irony was that it was an ideal time to set up a new band, as several key players such as Graham Nash (The Hollies) and Ginger Baker (The Small Faces) were now unattached. There was change in the air. It was, coincidentally, the beginning of the supergroup era.

Korner, who it will be remembered had been contacted by Jagger and Richards, was genuinely keen to do something to help. So assisting Jones with a new group seemed the way forward, even though he must have realized that, in Brian's present state, this might never happen and that he was witnessing the decline of his old friend which, possibly even without the presence of Thorogood, may have been in its terminal stages. It was very sad.

At first it looked as if this proposal might work with Brian. His ego boosted, he started getting in contact with a number of performers and producers to try and make the thing happen. He also set up a rehearsal studio at Cotchford. He even contacted John Lennon, who apparently expressed some interest in the project. Whether Lennon was just being polite to an old friend we do not know but he must have been aware of Brian's downward spiral. The problem was that the more people he got in touch with, the more the existing Stones came to hear of Brian's plans on the grapevine. There is no doubt that this set in motion his eventual termination from the band. But Korner, who may have unwittingly facilitated this, was just glad to see Brian actually playing again.

Cotchford Farm – The Dark Side

Saturday, June 9th 1969 was the day it happened, the day when Jagger and Richards decided that enough was enough and that, for the future of The Stones to be secured, they decided to be shot of Brian. They got into their cars with Charlie Watts that evening and the trio headed for Cotchford. When they arrived, Brian opened the door himself and it must have been obvious to him, at that point, what was about to happen. They explained to him that with regard to the forthcoming American tour, there was no way that the American authorities would allow Brian in because of his well-documented history of drug taking. At the same time Brian explained that he was no longer interested in going back on the road. Giuliano describes the scene.

> After a few uneventful minutes of small talk there was a painful lull in the conversation into which Richards inserted: 'Brian, you're out of the band. You're fired.'

> Brian smiled weakly saying nothing. (104, 1994)

And yet, as Nicholas Fitzgerald very properly points out in his book (1985), Jagger and Richards were not actually in a position to fire him. Brian had formed the group and there was no contract between them. So, while one can understand the group's need to be rid of him, I am a little doubtful about Giuliano's account of what went on in this meeting.

It seemed a little cruel of Mick Jagger to add that they had already found a substitute in the form of Mick Taylor (from The Bluesbreakers) who, apparently, was just waiting to step in. Everything had been worked out in advance. They also informed Brian that he would never be allowed into the States because of his drug history, which was true. Brian muttered something about it being probably the best thing for now but it still must have come as a hammer blow, to be removed from the band that he formed, especially when it was now so unbelievably successful. Even so, even in Brian's reduced state it can hardly have come as a surprise. After all, if he had thought he was remaining with The Stones, why was he contacting everyone who was anyone in the music world about forming a new band? The problem had always been Brian himself and his inability to control himself and it seems likely that many of those he contacted, while appearing enthusiastic, would by now have been aware of his decidedly

Semi-Detached Suburban Mr Jones

dodgy reputation and failure to deliver. This might have made them wary of commitment.

Jagger was then keen to try and leaven the shock by saying that Brian could, for the duration, still make use of the London office and that, of course, there would be a final payment of perhaps a hundred grand, one hell of a lot of money in 1969, and money that he probably never received because, just one short month later, he was dead. Whether that financial offer had any basis in reality or was just a way of easing Brian out we shall never know. For The Stones it was a hard-headed business decision, nothing else. They just wanted to be totally rid of Jones from the band but certainly not to hound him. This is backed up by the fact that he was, in the interim period, given the chance to make use of their office in London for help should he need it. This included the press office which might be able to offer Jones other opportunities. Even so, Charlie Watts considers The Stones' dismissal of Brian was too sudden:

> But I felt even sorrier for him, for what we did to him. We took his
> one thing away, which was being in a band. (108, 1994)

Brian was worried about what the press might say, and it was suggested that one way out was to claim that he was resigning because of 'musical differences', whatever that might mean. What it suggests is that Brian wanted to take the group in a direction that they did not want to go, keeping in mind that they had found great success with the kind of music that they were currently turning out.

Jim Carter-Fea was then manager of the Revolution Club. He moved in with Brian for a couple of weeks to look after him. By this time Brian had reached a new low and was emotionally drained. He just could not accept his sacking. And, rather than point his life in a new direction, he remained stuck in time, unable to move forward.

> On one occasion, Jones and Carter-Fea rolled up in front of the
> Olympic Studios at about 4.30am. Inside, Brian's old band was
> rocking away the small hours cutting their new album ... "They're in
> there making music and they don't want me." (106, 1994)

Then they drove slowly back towards Cotchford.

But Jagger and Richards had not entirely finished with Jones. They wanted to keep him well away from the music business and the media for a while so that Mick Taylor could be absorbed into the group, smoothly and successfully. This was needed for both their forthcoming US tour and the commercial success of their new single, *Honky Tonk Women*.

After that visit, according to Giuliano:

> After they left Brian bolted the door and beckoning his dogs to his side, he wept bitterly for the next four hours. (106, 1994)

If he was alone and entirely without witnesses, how could Giuliano have known that? While what he actually did may never be known, what Giuliano said is surely no more than surmise.

It is important to understand that what The Stones did to Brian that night was really inevitable, he had become so unreliable and, far from being leader, he was contributing very little to the band. The group could no longer go on the road with him, either in the UK or the US, because Brian Jones was a liability, a druggy who dragged the group down. Yet certain people did think it was a remarkably cruel way for Jagger and Richards to treat him. Marianne Faithfull's ex-husband, John Dunbar, explains:

> It was a really terrible thing they did to Brian. They had a lot of other options than to sack him as cruelly as that. They took away whatever last reserves Brian had. (105, 2016)

The problem is Dunbar did not explain what those options might be and it is almost impossible to see what other alternative would have been feasible. That night, a stiff announcement from The Stones' press office made it public and though it was attributed to Brian, it was certainly not written by him. Later Mick Jagger issued what seemed like a sincere and caring statement but he never showed as much to Brian when he was with him. It stated, quite untruthfully, that they had parted amicably and were still on excellent terms. Nothing could have been further from the truth. Brian was now, apparently, a broken man.

There is here a parallel to be drawn with Thorogood's similar treatment of Jones. Jagger and Jones never really got on but there may have been

Semi-Detached Suburban Mr Jones

another unspoken reason: Jagger's possible jealousy of Jones' success with women. At this time Brian was not really contributing to the band, only unfinished songs that could not be used because he could not be bothered to see things through. In addition, Cotchford Farm, supposed to be his saving grace, became just another backdrop for his neuroses. This in turn led to an even greater dependency on alcohol. His drug usage was mostly in the past but it was simply replaced by the demon drink. Brian Jones could not manage without support from one of these two sources. In one so young this seems desperately sad but Jones, despite being talented, was irredeemably weak. So much so that Jones, the owner of Cotchford Farm, became almost the servant to the wicked Thorogood who, far from keeping to his remit as a builder, completely took over. This meant that he and his men brought Cotchford, a highly respectable area, into disrepute by using it as a site for wild drinking and extra marital affairs. Mary Hallett was appalled and even Brian became embarrassed by what she had to endure.

Immediately after his sacking, Brian spent much time in his old haunts in London close to where The Stones practised. It was a kind of miserabilist gesture to be close to where he had once been part of the team. He was often drunk and mixing with the wrong kind of people just for companionship. I do not, for one moment, think that The Stones had anything in mind other than the secure future of the band, even if their way of achieving it had the air of a blunt instrument about it. However, the scurrilous Thorogood appears to have thought that, by undermining Brian at every turn, he was doing the bidding of The Stones. But there is no sign of any justification for this except possibly in the questionable role of the late Tom Keylock, and certainly no sign that The Stones suggested he behave in this manner. It is quite possible that, being of a sadistic nature, he quite simply enjoyed it.

> When Alexis [Korner] heard the news of Brian's sacking, he was concerned for his old friend. Fearful that his dismissal would crush him completely and undo all their weeks of good work, he and Bobbie went to see Brian the following day. They were amazed to see how calmly he had taken it. Instead of finding him, as they expected, in a state of mourning, Brian was in a good frame of mind. He was chirpy and eager to rehearse. He was also sober. Alex

98

believed him when he said he hadn't felt so good in years. (103, 2016)

This goes totally against what Giuliano suggested with Brian crying in a corner and implies that a worrying weight had been lifted from him. Yet Brian was up and down all the time, moving from misery to exhilaration very quickly.

Rawlings and Spendel go on to tell us how Brian, now totally free of The Stones' commitments, put his heart and soul into setting up the new group that Korner had suggested to him. He arranged an appointment with journalist Peter Jones to discuss how the group was going to go back to real rock and roll rather than the commercial stuff that The Stones had settled for. To his advantage, Brian still had the use of The Stones' office which was a tremendous help with his plans.

> As rehearsals got under way, and the likes of John Mayall, Mitch Mitchell and Steve Winwood pulled up at the farm, Brian's confidence soared. When they weren't jamming or playing, Brian either locked himself away in the small oak panelled studio or walked through the gardens of Cotchford blowing loudly on his saxophone, a habit that greatly annoyed Michael Martin. (105, 2016)

This was to prove yet another false dawn and virtually the last time that Brian behaved in any normal fashion. He was still being totally selfish but at least he seemed to be happy about it. But Brian's mood changed abruptly and he looked scared, a mood that seemed to dominate the last few days of his life. After all, there was just one short month left for him to live.

SPOTLIGHT:
ANITA PALLENBERG

Anita Pallenberg (1942–2017) was of Italian/German descent. Wikipedia (2024) tells us that her father was connected to the Cologne-based Pallenberg family dynasty. She was an actress, artist and model and the muse of The Rolling Stones. She first came across the band in 1965 and soon started a relationship with Brian Jones. Two years later she broke up with him after he assaulted her and transferred her affections to Keith Richards, with whom she had three children.

She was expelled from school at 16 after which she went to both Rome and New York where she mixed in with the Andy Warhol crowd. She appeared in a dozen films including *Barbarella* (1969), the German *A Degree of Murder* (1967) and *Performance* (1968). Distributor Warner Bros were shocked by the latter's content and delayed its release. Despite her ability and intelligence she seemed to exercise a baleful influence over The Stones, and was reputed to have practised black music, not to mention an interest in drugs.

Scott Cantrell, a groundsman, was just 17 when, on 20th July 1979, he shot himself in the head with a gun owned by Keith Richards in Salem, New York. He was in Pallenberg's bed at the time while Richards was away. The verdict was listed as a suicide.

In later life, she suffered from hepatitis C (a virus of the liver) and had a hip replacement after which she walked with a limp. She had been free of drugs for 14 years in 2014 when she had a relapse. A similar story applies to her alcohol consumption on which she was also an addict and attended AA meetings. Like Brian Jones, she seems to have wasted her undoubted talent and when asked by Alain Elkann in a 2016 interview about her life she said:

> I am ready to die. I have done so much here. My mum died at 94.
> I don't want to lose my independence. Now I am over 70 and to be
> honest I did not think I would live over 40.

Spotlight: Anita Pallenberg

She died on 13th June 2017 at the age of 75 and was buried in Worthing, West Sussex after a full but not necessarily a properly fulfilled life. In many ways she resembles a female version of Jones, initially talented but intent on wasting herself with all the worst influences. A new film, *The Story of Anita Pallenberg* (2024) fills in most of the details.

WHEN BLUE TURNS TO GREY

To start with it looked as if Brian had finally turned a corner.

> It was a jubilant Brian, that opened the door to Mrs Hallett a couple of days later. "We're alright now," he told her. "My money is coming through from America." "I remember it clearly," she says. "It was the same day there was a story in the paper about Mick Jagger." The *News of the World* were running an article about Jagger's recent drug bust in London. Mick and Marianne Faithfull had been arrested at their house in Cheyne Walk and charged with possession of a quarter of an ounce of hash and a quantity of heroin by the very officer, Detective Sergeant Norman Pilcher and his team of detectives that had done such a splendid job on Brian. "Brian was laughing like a drain when he heard the news on the radio." (105/6, 2016)

How times had changed. Just when things were bad for The Stones, it looked as if the ever fickle Brian was in the ascendant. But it was only very temporary.

It is worth pointing out that Tom Keylock was no longer The Stones' roadie having been assigned the task of looking after Brian. So he was constantly visiting Cotchford to check on how the renovations were getting on. Technically he was supposed to be supervising the work on behalf of The Stones' office but, if that were the case, Keylock was not doing a very good job. Only slow progress was being made and any work which was alleged to have been completed was not of a good standard. Thorogood and his men were much too busy enjoying their billet at Cotchford and playing away with their various mistresses. However, since Brian had been removed from the band, the workmen were concerned that they might not receive their wages and Keylock had to assure them that, despite recent events, there was no problem in that area. But the builders were continuing to make waves.

> Michael Martin overheard Frank telling Tom that Mrs Hallett should go. Mrs Hallett made no secret of the fact that she didn't like

When Blue Turns To Grey

Keylock or any of the builders and wasted little time in telling them so at every opportunity. "I knew they weren't real builders." (106, 2016)

Thorogood was aware that Mary Hallett was very close to Brian, and was doing his best to break that connection so that he could isolate Jones. But Mrs Hallett, whilst she was well aware of Brian's many faults, was one of the few people he got on with and was no pushover. The mixture was being stirred to boiling point.

One of the reasons was that The Stones' office, fully aware of his sudden departure from the band, was not going to keep allowing Brian to sponge off them for very long. Nothing Jagger had told Jones was in writing and The Stones' accountants began to demand the very cutbacks that Thorogood and his men thought might happen. It was only common sense and they certainly did not want to pay for this ongoing and apparently much delayed and expensive building work to continue. The days of his dissolute lifestyle were obviously numbered and although it was not Brian's decision, he was the one who was likely to get the blame because he was on the spot and the builders (and their various mistresses) would have to look for pastures new.

It was quite remarkable just how close Brian had got to Mary Hallett. According to Rawlings and Spendel:

> She had become a surrogate mother figure and confidante to him. He had even installed her phone so that that he could call her at all times of the day and night and he paid every bill. "Shall I tell you what I think it was," she explained. "My son was killed when he was twenty-three by a car and after Brian moved in and he was around a similar age. In a way he gave me back something which I had lost." (106, 2016)

For Brian it was almost a mirror image of his own disastrous home life, losing his sister so very young. Mary had belatedly become the reliable parent that he had never had. It was pathetic and yet at the same time rather charming that, so late in his short life, Brian had finally found someone on which he could depend. All the bad behaviour for which he had become famous disappeared when he was with Mary, and he became once again

Semi-Detached Suburban Mr Jones

the middle-class son from Cheltenham. But this was only an oasis in a very large desert.

The builders absolutely hated this situation and their behaviour became ever more bizarre, leading to a series of unpleasant confrontations that Keylock, who was supposed to be supervising them, couldn't or wouldn't stop. It was very much in Thorogood's interest to have Mary removed. After all, if there were going to be cutbacks, she could be a very useful example of savings to The Stones' office. And yet curiously, Thorogood stopped short of addressing her directly.

> "They didn't like me around. It unnerved them," she stated. "If they saw me coming down the path, I would hear them say, 'Quick, Mrs Hallett is coming'." (106, 2016)

The result of all this was that Mary's wages were cut, something that can only have been arranged by Tom Keylock in cahoots with Thorogood. They were trying to wear her down. It was disgraceful and when Brian eventually got to hear about it, he immediately had the matter put right. This extended to three cats that Mary had taken on from previous owners, the Taylors, who were cruelly treated by the builders and kicked around. Ridiculously she was told to give them cheaper food. The builders took every opportunity to try and get rid of Mary as well, but it didn't work. She was made of sterner stuff and she was not going to leave Brian. So, to ensure the cats were safe, she took them back to her home so they would not be abused by the builders. It is also disgraceful that Tom Keylock, so previously efficient, did absolutely nothing to stop this dissolute behaviour.

Worse still, Rawlings tells us that Mary Hallett reported:

> One morning when I was at the sink, Mo came up behind me and stood really close. He started being very rude and rubbing himself against me, so I turned round quick as you like and emptied a packet of Flash down his trousers. I kept away for a while after that. (106, 2016)

Things were reaching a dangerous pitch and, as Michael Martin said:

> Up until this point Brian had been too easy-going and had not paid enough attention to what was going on. He started to have his say but he sort of still half trusted them. He couldn't see that things were

When Blue Turns To Grey

getting out of hand. [More likely that he could but he didn't have the courage to do anything about it.] They were taking outrageous liberties with him. Mo threatened to fill me in if I made a fuss about what I saw them doing. (107, 2016)

Michael had a quiet word with Brian anyway and Brian, making use of previously learned skills, rigged up a hidden speaker system in the public areas so that he could hear what the builders were up to when he was in his bedroom. But knowing what they were about and doing something about it were two very different things.

Still pining after Anita Pallenberg, Brian took up with yet another foreign girlfriend to replace Suki Potier. This was the Swedish Anna Wohlin who, in June 1969, moved into Cotchford. Keylock was very angry about this new connection and wanted Brian to drop her, but he refused. Yet because of the amount of time he spent playing she, like so many before her, just became part of the furniture with Brian's attention devoted to his music and forthcoming new band. He attempted to keep her apart from Frank's men whose moral code came from the gutter. However, this latest acquisition seemed like a bad idea as, according to Mrs Hallett:

> She didn't make Brian happy. She would wander around the house in front of the builders in one of those crochet string-vest type dresses, which you could see right through, and the little devil never wore anything underneath. (107, 2016)

One can imagine the effect this had on the already oversexed builders, Mo and Johnny. Looking back, it seems almost impossible to believe the depths to which Cotchford Farm had sunk due almost entirely to Frank Thorogood and his men and the total failure of Tom Keylock to stop it.

And then we come to something rather important, although it did not seem to be so at the time. Frank Thorogood, behaving more and more like a would-be lord of the manor, hired girlfriend Joan Fitzsimons, a minicab driver, as his chauffeur. In fact she was there at Thorogood's pleasure but he was prepared to justify it by offering her to Brian as occasional driver. Keep her name in mind, as it is an intriguing part of the puzzle to which we shall return.

Semi-Detached Suburban Mr Jones

Added to this already potent mix was Helen Colby (née Spittal), a teenage Stones groupie who Brian took a fancy to and who visited him at Cotchford. He told her about his plans for the new band and also showed her round the house and gardens, introducing her to Anna along the way. He seemed very proud of it all.

> Then Brian's mood changed and he whispered to Helen while looking out of the window at Frank. "He pointed to Frank and told me he was supposed to be a builder, but he never did anything. He said he was lazy. I said, 'Why don't you sack him?' and he just mumbled. I watched Frank after that because Brian kept on about him and he did absolutely nothing all day. There was no sign of any construction work going on at all. He was just wandering around like part of the scenery." (108, 2016)

Helen's time at Cotchford was more of an education than she could have possibly conceived. She had believed that Brian had left the band voluntarily and it wasn't till he made some obtuse comment to her that she began to realize he had been deliberately pushed out. The Stones were putting on a free gig in Hyde Park on 5th July 1969, and Helen asked Brian if he was going but he declined saying that Anita would be there. It was then obvious to Helen that, even after all this time, he still pined for her, perhaps the only girlfriend out of all of them that he really cared for. The rest were just there to amuse him and they never really got close to Brian. This was even true of the Anita substitute, Anna, who despite her obvious sex appeal, just didn't cut the mustard as far as Brian was concerned. So, while Brian's brief life had been full of opportunities, very few of them had actually worked out, leaving him with disappointments and a sea of heartache for others. Helen Spittal, incidentally, took what turned out to be the last few photographs of Jones before he died.

Meanwhile, Brian was now very much overweight, not due to eating too much, but because of his incessant drinking. However, he didn't usually appear to be drunk. The hedonistic years had taken their toll and he was now a confirmed alcoholic.

> A loud knock at the door interrupted Helen's thoughts and she watched as Anna went to answer it ... It was Jackie [Joan],

When Blue Turns To Grey

> Thorogood's cab-driving mistress, who had arrived from London.
> She handed Brian a little bottle of pills, which Brian was keen to
> show Helen were on prescription. (109, 2016)

So, the medical dependence that had been such a source of laughter amongst The Stones was continuing. Throughout his life and despite periods of bluster to the contrary, Brian was a little lost boy dependent not just on potions, people and their applause and but also on drink and drugs. He had become hopelessly inadequate. Yet he realized he was going to be in big trouble with The Stones' office if he did not take action against Thorogood and his men who were now into cruel japes such as hiding Brian's scooter and even running up colossal bills ordering themselves furniture as if Cotchford was *their* home. They assumed that Brian would be too spaced out to do anything about them and so they went on taking the most diabolical liberties. But on that day, he was not. It was 2nd July 1969. Far from doing any meaningful construction, they were actually intent on leaving the sort of mess that only builders can dream up. Ironically, this was no doubt to justify them staying on.

On the morning of 2nd July, Mary Hallett found the builders in the kitchen finishing breakfast and told them she wanted them out of there but they didn't move. Making her mop wringing wet she then decided to soak the men, who were furious with her. It was a strangely symbolic act and prescient of what was to come later that evening. Brian's asthma was particularly bad but he seemed in reasonable spirits because he had heard Mary's *contretemps* with the builders on the intercom system he had set up.

In addition, he had asked Michael Martin if he could attend his regular Bible class in Crowborough to warn the attendees that he was a good example of how not to lead a young life. He wanted to warn them off. In retrospect, it shows Brian up as a person of extremes; leading a hedonistic lifestyle yet knowing the Bible in great depth and regularly quoting from it. In this respect he seems redolent of Mark Twain's concept of the human soul, suspended as it were between the two banks of a river representing good and evil, and the river being the course of one's life, making its way slowly to life's end at the sea.

Semi-Detached Suburban Mr Jones

July 2nd was a busy day and started with the return of Suki Potier, still vainly trying to retrieve the situation with Brian although deep down she must have known it was hopeless. Although she had returned before from time to time, this was the last time she would see him. Suki was followed to Cotchford later by a group of girls who were keen to see where Brian lived. They were invited in and wandered through the grounds mixing with all and sundry, including the builders. It was a strange day, almost as if the players were all assembled on stage for the third and deadly final act.

SPOTLIGHT:
ALEXIS KO[E]RNER (1928–1984)

Alexis Korner was an influential musician who specialized in British blues, hence the attraction for Brian Jones whose one musical aim was to popularize the blues, not only in terms of its British adaptation, but also in bringing out the original American style for British audiences. Once we understand this, it is easier to understand the rift that grew between himself and the rest of The Stones who were more interested in honing a commercial product than the purist blues version that Brian sought.

Korner was a major influence on the British music scene in the 1960s and, being some 14 years older than Brian, he was just the man to school this unruly talent on what it takes to be a band member of note. Korner was born in Paris to a Jewish father and a mother of mixed Greek, Turkish and Austrian descent. As a result, there was always something slightly exotic about him. Boogie-woogie pianist Jimmy Yancey convinced him that the blues was the way to go in the UK, as well as being an original step for the time. So it is easy to understand how Brian Jones became a soulmate. In 1961, just when Jones was waking up to the possibilities of music in the newly established coffee bars of Cheltenham and elsewhere, Korner and Cyril Davies formed Blues Incorporated from an eclectic range of musicians who shared a love of both pure blues and the rhythm and blues discipline. While Davies left the group in 1962, many other well-known musicians played with the band for a while as well as Brian Jones, so its makeup was less than fixed. Even Mick Jagger and Keith Richards had occasionally been part of his line-up. Many of these guest musicians started their own bands, such as The Rolling Stones, and Korner was eventually eclipsed by the success of these which left him as a kind of founding father, whose wide musical knowledge gave him the authority to broadcast regularly on the subject. He was much respected by his peers and especially by Jones as a demanding but also kind and generous friend.

Semi-Detached Suburban Mr Jones

Fast forward to 1969 and Jones' brief tenure at Cotchford Farm. At this time Korner was forming the band New Church and it was this group that Jones, down on his uppers after having been expelled from The Stones, wanted to join. But by this time, he had become both an alcoholic and a liability and could not be taken on. New Church were one of the support bands at The Rolling Stones' concert in Hyde Park on 5th July 1969, the very month of Jones' untimely death.

Korner married Roberta Melville (aka Bobbie), daughter of an art critic and had two sons and a daughter. He and his family visited Jones at Cotchford a couple of times to try and help him with future plans and to some extent they did, albeit they were short-lived. Korner died in January 1984 of lung cancer, smoking being a particular hazard in his line of country. He was just 55.

THIS COULD BE THE LAST TIME

I thought long and hard about how to tackle the events of 2nd July 1969. The reason is that all who were involved that night are now dead and it is therefore impossible to establish precisely what happened or who did what to whom and when. It all boils down to a short period of a few hours that July evening when Jones met his end. Even more important is the most fundamental question: Was it an accident or was Cotchford Farm on that summer evening a crime scene? The police firmly believe the former and state there was no evidence for anything else. Yet, just as in the more recent Barrymore case in 2001, there has been a suggestion that the investigation was not as thorough as it ought to have been. The cases have similarities in that they both involved a male death in a swimming pool and both involved celebrities with a distinct possibility of drug taking. Also, both appear to have involved a cover-up by the parties concerned countered with what appears to be a certain reluctance by the police to get at the truth. In the Barrymore case the crime scene may have been initially improperly secured so that evidence may have been tampered with, either accidentally or on purpose. There appears to have been a certain reluctance from on high to release certain information to the public. Exactly why is not clear.

In one case the celebrity died. In the other he merely fled the scene. While Barrymore has more recently admitted to being gay which may or may not be relevant to what happened, Brian Jones was definitely not, despite aforementioned allegations of cross dressing and misinterpretations of this by other journalists. Of course, any incident of this sort is likely to cause problems in terms of what the public should be told and top policemen are, unsurprisingly, political animals and sometimes operate on a surprisingly different level to that which the public might expect.

What happened next bears some striking similarities in this case to the one at entertainer Michael Barrymore's (Michael Ciaran Parker) home on March 31st 2001. After meeting Barrymore at a local public house, Stuart

Lubbock, his brother and others went to the entertainer's home. Stuart, just a young man with no previous record, was found dead by the swimming pool and there was some suspicion he had been raped. He had no previous association with drugs, of which there was some evidence. Just as after the death of Brian Jones, the police investigation there met with a wall of silence apart from pre-prepared evidence from those present. Barrymore was detained on suspicion of rape and murder but later released. He sued Essex Police but got nothing. There, just as at Cotchford Farm, there was evidence of drug taking. It appeared that Lubbock died of drowning and there was alcohol in his body. According to the *Watford Observer*:

> Essex coroner Caroline Beasley-Murray heard how factory
> supervisor Mr Lubbock, from Harlow, had taken a cocktail of drugs,
> including cocaine, amphetamine and ecstasy. (2002)

While the case put an end to Barrymore's career, no satisfactory conclusion came about and nobody was ever charged with Lubbock's murder. Just as with the death of Brian Jones, the rumours continued to circulate. The wall of silence that surrounds these deaths was either brought about by threats if any party revealed anything useful or by fear of reprisals for illegal drug taking, assault or any combination of the above. The saddest thing in both cases is that there is no closure for the families of the dead, the players in these dramas putting their own safety, perhaps understandably, above any such considerations. It leaves a nasty taste and gives the opportunity for countless journalists to rake over the coals for years afterwards to ever diminishing effect. However, in March 2021 the police made an arrest in the Lubbock case, so hopefully this may eventually lead to closure for his family.

So, my answer to the reader is to present a series of scenarios backed up in some cases by circumstantial evidence in order that you can work out which you believe to be the most likely. But it does seem to me, especially in the light of what happened afterwards, that one scenario is more likely than the others. It carries just that bit more weight. What we do know is there has been an awful lot of print expended in the past 50 years on speculation as to what really happened. Much of it is repetitive but some of it contains a few nuggets of useful material that may offer clues to the truth.

This Could Be The Last Time

What we can be pretty certain of is that while the other Stones justifiably wanted Brian removed from the band, they were not in any way involved in what happened that evening. The way that Brian was evicted may have been unnecessarily cruel but they knew that he was no longer a useful, contributing member of the band. Also, just as Korner unwittingly facilitated Jones' removal, the actual sacking gave Thorogood extra ammunition in his ongoing intimidation of Brian Jones.

Among these are some things that it is impossible to ignore. For example, there is no question that Tom Keylock's old schoolfriend, Frank Thorogood, was present on the night in question and that he had, early on in his time at Cotchford, begun a campaign of intimidation against Brian Jones. Keylock's girlfriend, nurse Janet Lawson, was also there. It is alleged that Thorogood periodically locked Brian out of Cotchford, stole some money and other goods from Brian where they were carelessly left around, and played fast and loose with his booze while totally failing to complete any useful work. He and his team of undesirables used Cotchford as a personal playground for themselves and their mistresses. It surprises me that Mary Hallett and Michael Martin, who had both threatened to leave when Brian moved in, were prepared to put up with it for as long as they did but, of course, the whole tenure was only seven months. The irony was that the very London deadbeats that Brian had condemned when he first arrived at Cotchford were now present at the farm in the shape of the builders. And they were far worse. The longer they stayed, the tenser the atmosphere. We should remember that at this point Brian belonged to no band. He was in limbo, no longer part of The Stones but still somehow dependent on them and nowhere near sufficiently advanced with the proposed new group for it to have become a reality. He was on his own in a way he had not been since he was a child, and he was overstretched financially. As yet there was no settlement from The Stones and the only money he was due was residuals from his previous employment. The misplaced concept was that, because he was living at Cotchford and still had a chauffeur, he must be very wealthy but the truth was otherwise. He was actually in debt. In addition, Brian had never had any idea how to control himself with money, as indeed with anything else. It slipped away as fast as it came in. So the assumption by Thorogood that he must have loads of money, apparently evidenced by what cash he left lying around, was incorrect.

At this point, Brian was decidedly isolated which Alex Korner had noted on his visit. Brian, because of the builders, was far from master of his own house. He had known some dark times in his life, but none was darker than the situation that existed on 2nd July 1969. Yet, for all the promise and skill he had shown as a child, he had utterly failed to meaningfully promote himself, this despite his very real instrumental skills.

The Hallett family lived just down the lane from Cotchford and unfortunately, because of the acoustics in the area, any music or partying there seemed to be taking place in their own back garden. The possibility of a restful evening that summer night seemed to be completely out of the question. What they could not possibly have known was that it would be the last time they would be disturbed in that manner.

> Suddenly, the sounds of good natured partying changed. Mary listened. "There was a terrific lot of screaming coming from down there, awful screaming noises and then car doors slamming and engines going and cars screeching away." (110, 2016)

This is particularly significant because it could have been part of a cover-up to have deliberately reduced the number of people who were present on that fateful night. Mary despatched her husband Les to see what was going on but after all the cars had left, there was only an ominous silence. She also describes hearing a strange crackling noise quite late into the evening which she could not identify. It could have been a fire but there was no smoke.

The following day, after those strange events, the news came in that Brian Jones had died in the swimming pool. The Halletts were deeply shocked and only found out through Michael Martin, who had heard it from a friend. Certainly the press had got hold of it very fast. It seemed extraordinary that the unpredictable wild child from Cheltenham had reached the end of his short life at just 27. And yet, it may have been in the stars: living the kind of life he did and at the speed he did so. He packed more into those few years than many people do in a lifetime, even if it was interspersed with drink and drugs. He could never have lived to middle age because he was already burnt out.

This Could Be The Last Time

As Mary Hallett headed for Cotchford, she was intercepted by Tom Keylock who escorted her to the farmhouse. He now seemed to be trying to control matters very carefully and this continued for a long time following Brian's death.

> It was then she heard for the second time, the same crackling noise she had heard the previous night. But now she was able to identify the source of the alien crackle. It was police walkie-talkies. (111, 2016)

But the point is, was the swimming pool a crime scene or was what happened an unfortunate but entirely natural death? In order to try and get at the truth, we need to examine several different scenarios.

Scenario I: A Natural Death

From what we know of Brian at that time, he was overweight and his asthma was playing him up the previous day. This was confirmed by the coroner. We also know that he was drinking far too much at that time. As to whether he had taken any drugs that evening, the jury is out. The reason for that is because the witness statements given to the police by the various people there that evening lack consistency. It isn't even possible to say with any certainty exactly how many people were there at Cotchford the previous evening and the screeching tyres of cars leaving the farm that Mary Hallett heard are an indicator of that. Between Brian's passing and the arrival of the police, Keylock and Thorogood had the opportunity to cook up a story about what happened, to enforce it with everyone present there and to swiftly exit everyone else.

Janet Lawson, according to Giuliano, claimed that:

> Brian Jones visited the [garage] flat about 10.30pm on the Wednesday evening and invited my friend and I to join him at the house. We did so and Brian guided us back to the house with a hand torch. It was clear that he was unsteady on his feet as the light was unreliable. He seemed to be talking quite sensibly, I believe about the drainage scheme. Nevertheless it was obvious that he had been drinking.

Semi-Detached Suburban Mr Jones

> My friend and I sat at the dining-room table and drinks were there, but
> I did not take it. Brian and my friend were drinking spirits. (127, 1994)

In addition to this, Brian reported that he had taken his 'sleepers' or sleeping tablets. Lawson goes on to describe how Anna, Frank and Brian had decided to go swimming. So if we put all this together and add the asthma, Brian was in no fit state to swim. Yet we are told despite this that Brian was a very able, even acrobatic swimmer. So if we are to believe the coroner's verdict on what happened to him, then it was merely a case of death by misadventure; a euphemism in this case perhaps for a combination of asthma, drink and drugs. But we do know that Thorogood was at the pool with him and Anna went inside to take a telephone call.

At the time of his demise, Jones was in very poor shape. Also we know that his asthma was particularly bad that day. It would have been unsurprising that his late-night swim turned into a disaster, especially since he had to be helped to stand upright on the diving board. We could accept all of that except for the ominous presence of Frank Thorogood, who we know was at loggerheads with Brian, and, according to Lawson, was behaving quite strangely. When he was dragged out of the pool, Anna Wohlin claimed that he still had a pulse but when the doctors arrived there was no sign of life.

Dick Hattrell, Jones' much abused but ever loyal friend, had this to say about him:

> I feel since Brian left The Stones he would have lived only a matter
> of weeks unless he had quickly found his full potential. He was on
> the down road. There was always a sense of doom about him and he
> was under a psychiatrist's care for years. (194, 1994)

I think this is a fair assessment since, given his lack of songwriting skills, he was forced to play the commercial music of Jagger and Richards rather than what he would have chosen. This may have earned him money but, as we have seen, his heart was not in it while with The Stones.

Scenario 2: A Deliberate Drowning

Tom Keylock had allegedly been asked to deliver a guitar to The Stones at Olympic Studios in London that evening. By this time in the game, Frank

This Could Be The Last Time

Thorogood had every reason to object to Jones who, by his very sacking from The Stones, would be likely to end his increasingly cushy contract at Cotchford. He was also contemptuous of Jones as a weak and paranoid individual who deserved whatever was dished out to him. The fact that Thorogood's work was at best shoddy and at worst almost non-existent didn't come into it. The guiding factor was that most people whom Thorogood came into contact with realized he was incompetent but were wary about standing up to such a threatening and unpleasant individual.

But the problem is that Frank Thorogood states that Brian Jones was watching television with him a good hour before the time claimed by Lawson; 9.30 p.m. rather than 10.30 p.m. In addition, the waters are muddied by the number of people at Cotchford that evening because Brian had invited people to a party. Amongst these were alleged to be the designer Elan, a member of the Walker Brothers and a friend of Brian's, Nicholas Fitzgerald. Rather than being specifically invited, the heir to the Guinness fortune had first been rung by Suki Potier who felt Brian was at risk and later by a Ralph Hampton who said that Jones wanted to see him. Brian knew Fitzgerald from his previous connection with the Irish family.

Nicholas Fitzgerald and his student friend, Richard Cadbury, despite previous requests, were undecided as to whether to visit Cotchford that evening, but finally did so, arriving at about 11.15 p.m. According to Giuliano:

> They see a foreign car (with the headlights on) blocking the drive to Brian's house. The driver's door is open and the motor is running. (221, 1994)

It looks poised for a quick getaway. In view of this, they make their way to Brian's property via the Bluebell Wood.

> There, through the bushes, they glimpse the pool brightly lit with the newly installed spotlights. Moving forward they observe Brian being held underwater by three men. (221, 1994)

Apparently, author Giuliano obtained confirmation of this from one of the three but doesn't say who. Nicholas Fitzgerald's own book, *Brian Jones: The Inside story of the Original Rolling Stone* (1985) tells the story as follows. And, as Fitzgerald and Cadbury were the only witnesses, I want to

Semi-Detached Suburban Mr Jones

go back to the source material but at the same time issue a caveat. There is something novelettish about Fitzgerald's account that makes it read more like something he made up rather than something that actually happened. There is also the presence of his asthma, which he shared with Jones and, by his own admission, the mention of a number of substances in his book, the presence of which tend to offer a distraction from the truth. In short, the account of Brian Jones' death in the book seems strangely melodramatic. After emerging from Bluebell Wood, they entered the garden.

> We skirted the summer house, came around to its side and saw the full glare of the lights now over the pool and in the windows of the house. We were in a kind of twilight here at the corner of the summer house. We had a clear view of the pool and of what was going on there. And what the hell was going on?

> At the far right hand corner of the swimming pool three men were standing. They were dressed in sweaters and jeans. Their clothes gave the impression they were workmen. The power of the spotlights blotted out their features and made their faces look like white blobs. (240, 1985)

This last point seems remarkably convenient to avoid identifying witnesses. The interesting thing here is, where is Thorogood? Where did the three men come from and where, after the crime, did they go? They are not mentioned by anyone else, including Janet Lawson. Given that the spotlights were on full, they must have been fully obvious from the house.

> The moment I became aware of them, the middle one dropped to his knees, reached into the water and pushed down on the top of a head that looked white.

> At the opposite end of the pool – far left – stood two other people, a man and a woman, gazing down into the pool where the kneeling man was pushing down on the head, keeping it under. The man to the right of the kneeling man said something. It sounded like a command and I caught the words "… do something." At that, the third man on that side jumped into the water the way an animal might jump, arms outstretched, knees bent. He landed on the back of the struggling

This Could Be The Last Time

swimmer. The man who snapped out the command seemed to be preparing himself also to jump in. Breathless, unbelieving, paralyzed, I looked at the man and woman. She was standing a little in his shadow, and I couldn't see her face. But why didn't they move? Do something? They looked like extras on a film set, waiting to play their parts. Somebody had got to do something. (240, 1985)

It is at this point that Fitzgerald and Cadbury are accosted by whom we are later told is Tom Keylock but if he is supposedly up in London, delivering a guitar to Olympic Studios, how is this possible?

Since he is described as burly, could it be someone else altogether? Fitzgerald and Cadbury are grabbed and told:

"Get the hell out of here, Fitzgerald, or you'll be next," he growled. It was a cockney accent.

I was terrified. He meant it. There was no way I could do battle with him. He turned me around and pushed me hard in the back into the woods. I almost fell, but went stumbling blindly into the darkness under the trees. Ahead of me I heard the rustle and the swish as Cadbury went struggling away. I followed this sound, briars grasping my ankles like the claws of a cat, twigs and leaves brushing my face. I fell and hit a tree with my head. Some kind of creeper tried to entwine itself around my chest and waist. I broke free. Were there sounds behind me? *Please, God, no.*

And now I saw the lights of the parked car. I saw Cadbury climbing into mine. I got in beside him and I couldn't breathe. Asthma. I grabbed my inhaler and puffed too many times. My heart was pounding. Why wasn't the bloody car moving? Were those people out there searching for us with lights?

"Richard," I said. I looked at him. He was slumped over the steering wheel, groaning.

"What the hell's the matter?" I was almost shrieking. Shock, I told myself. I was in shock. "Get this bloody thing out of here!"

His hand trembled uncontrollably, but the engine revved up and we were flying backward, straight into the main road, the tyres

Semi-Detached Suburban Mr Jones

> screaming for mercy, then forward with a roar that should have
> woken the whole village. We were going the wrong way, on the road
> to Uckfield instead of London. But we were away from that damned
> place, away from those damned people. (241, 1985)

The rest of the account describes how they soon ran out of fuel and Cadbury went to look for some. In the meantime, Fitzgerald is picked up by a lorry driver, hoping to see Cadbury on the way. Instead he falls asleep and eventually is let out of the lorry at Battersea Bridge. Fitzgerald goes home to his apartment in Cheyne Walk, takes 'a lot of Valium tablets and collapsed on the bed'.

The curious thing is neither man appears to have considered calling the police. They were apparently simply concerned with their own skins.

Compare that with this account provided by Trevor Hobley from the Brian Jones Fan Club:

> Nic Fitzgerald made a verbal statement to a witness ... confirming
> that both himself and Cadbury saw three men holding a body upside
> down with the head in a trough of water. Bernard Toms however,
> ghost writing Fitzgerald's book states ... that the body was being
> held underwater in the swimming pool. (2005)

No, Fitzgerald did not say he 'saw three men holding a body upside down with the head in a trough of water'. There was no need for a trough if there was a swimming pool and was he really upside down? This appears to be some distortion of the truth.

But one of the Cotchford carpet fitters, David Gibson, who was working at the property, made a separate statement and was around in the days before Brian's death, knew he was terrified of something, just as he had expressed earlier. This fits in with a number of telephone calls made to friends, also sounding disturbed. Apparently they knew that he had made plans to go to a foreign location with a blonde, presumably Anna Wohlin, presumably with the idea of escaping abroad but he was just too late.

Was the man with the cockney accent who chased Fitzgerald and Cadbury off the property our old friend, Tom Keylock, now getting his hands decidedly

This Could Be The Last Time

dirty? It is possible that he may have known Thorogood's intention and that he had to keep Cotchford as clear of witnesses as possible. Keylock initially claimed that he was not there on the night in question but several witnesses remember seeing him and he eventually changed his story. Did he or did he not go to Olympic Studios in London that night? When we first met Tom Keylock, he seemed to be a tough yet efficient operator who was good for The Stones in terms of venue management. Yet by the time we reach 1969, sidelined by the band to keep an eye on Jones, he emerges as an altogether shadier character, quite clearly in cahoots with Frank Thorogood since otherwise, he would not have been allowed the freedom he was given to do, quite literally, whatever he liked without ever seriously attempting any building work. It is a strange phenomenon, how highly successful pop performers often attract the worst kind of assistants, cf. Tom Parker and Elvis. We know that Thorogood was ripping off Jones big-time but was Keylock? There is no hard evidence of it, but the possibility remains.

If Jones was known to be planning on going abroad, then this was the last chance for Thorogood to do something about him. In any event, he must have known that whatever happened from then on, his time at Cotchford was severely limited. And yet, there was the public image to be considered in the aftermath. Trevor Hobley suggests that:

> Even though lower-rank DCI Bob Marshall was woken at 2am to go and investigate Brian's death, it must be assumed that it had been pre-determined from somebody in authority that Brian Jones' death was going to be a death by 'misadventure'. (2005)

This is a little hard to accept. There may be all sorts of reasons why a more senior officer might not be despatched and, while celebrity deaths always carry a political aspect with them, it seems more likely that the outcome was decided on the basis of evidence, however flimsy. Anna Wohlin was probably intimidated by Thorogood and therefore her statement at the time may have been at best incomplete, and at worst, inaccurate. There are good reasons for supposing this as we will see when we come to examine the dreadful event that befell cab driver Joan Fitzsimons. Brian's death and its ramifications did not end on the night in question. It echoed down the following years in various ways. There would have been severe penalties

Semi-Detached Suburban Mr Jones

for those going against the accepted cover story. In this way, it is similar to the Barrymore case.

Of course, Brian was already known to the police in London as something of an undesirable in his association with drugs. And so we can assume that the investigating cops from East Sussex already knew much of Brian's background. With this in mind, if we think that the investigation was as some have suggested less than thorough, it is possible that the outcome 'death by misadventure' is not so surprising. A worthless person meeting a worthless end perhaps. Why bother to look further?

We already know that Brian's asthma was bad that day, but he had lost his inhaler and so, while by the swimming pool, he despatched Janet Lawson to look for it in the house. She thinks that this gave Thorogood the opportunity he was looking for. Scott Jones, interviewing Janet Lawson, shortly before she died of cancer, reports as follows:

> 'There was something in the air. Frank was acting strangely, throwing his weight about a bit. In the early evening Frank, Anna, Brian and myself had dinner – steak and kidney pie.'

> After eating, the group returned to the garden where Jones and Thorogood larked about in the pool. Later, when Jones was in the pool by himself, he asked Janet to find his asthma inhaler.

> 'I went to look for it by the pool, in the music room, the reception room and then the kitchen. Frank came in in a lather. His hands were shaking. He was in a terrible state. I thought the worst almost straight away and went to the pool to check.'

> 'When I saw Brian on the bottom of the pool and was calling for help, Frank initially did nothing.'

> 'I shouted for Frank again as I ran towards the house, and he burst out before I reached it, ran the pool and dived in. But I had not said where Brian was. I thought, "How did he know Brian was at the bottom of the pool?"'

> 'I ran back to the house and tried to call 999 but Anna was on the phone and would not get off it.' [In those circumstances would you not just grab the phone from her?]

122

This Could Be The Last Time

But, in her original statement, Janet did not mention the tension between Jones and Thorogood, or the fact that she feared the worst as soon as she saw Thorogood coming in from the pool.

Nor did she reveal how Thorogood initially ignored her cries for help or that he dived into the pool without her telling him that was where Jones was.

Did she think Thorogood had killed Jones?

'Yes.' (2008)

The problem is that this version conflicts with Fitzgerald's, who claimed that there were three men holding Brian underwater. Who were they and where did they come from and where did they go? They could have been Johnny, Mo and Dave, Thorogood's regular workmates. Brian Jones decided to go for a swim on the off chance, so any element of pre-planning seems unlikely. If something was done to him it surely had to be because an opportunity suddenly presented itself.

The whole of this account throws up questions about just who was on the premises that evening. It looks as if there were initially more than was revealed to the police because, by the time they got there, Keylock and Thorogood had the opportunity to do some clearing up and ensure that certain others had left the premises. Sanitized for your inconvenience perhaps. But a question mark remains over where Keylock was that evening, in London or at Cotchford, because the timings with Fitzgerald are out.

Scenario 3: Rendered Unconscious in the House

In his statement for the Brian Jones Fan Club, Trevor Hobley states that:

I tend to believe … that Brian might have been rendered unconscious in the house leading me to believe that there might still be a crime scene. (2005)

I find this possibility unlikely. There were surely just too many people about that evening to make that a practical hypothesis. It would have meant lugging the unconscious Jones all the way from the house to the swimming pool with its attendant difficulties. Also, what would be the point since two

Semi-Detached Suburban Mr Jones

or more men could easily overcome the alcoholic Jones. No, if something was done to harm Jones, I believe it was done in the close vicinity of the swimming pool.

Yes, Jones was a small man although, by this time, he was also overweight, as testified to in the autopsy. Mind you, this also refers to Jones as being 5′9″ tall, which he wasn't. The pathology report, created in 1969, refers to him being 5′11″ when he was no more than 5′6″. It seems extraordinary that such important analytical documents can get even the basics wrong. This, by implication, calls into question everything else contained therein.

One of the biggest problems that the police encountered was that in between the time that Brian Jones died and the police arriving, there was enough time for a cover story to be concocted sufficient to prevent anyone being caught in the frame. Mary Hallett has made it clear that she heard cars driving away from Cotchford at speed. Who was in them and why did they leave? The answer must be that their departure made it all the easier to support the cover story. Although Mary Hallett lived only just down the lane, the physical construction of Cotchford and its surrounds made up of so many trees and bushes dictated that what went on there would be largely private and hidden from outsiders. This of course explains Fitzgerald's and Cadbury's difficulty when approaching as well as explaining the appeal to the Milnes. It was pretty much a private world which became that of Pooh and Christopher Robin, but it should never have admitted the troubled Jones. Even though he wanted to inhabit their world and loved the characters portrayed by Milne, it is probably fair to say that even if he had not met his untimely end that July evening, it is unlikely that he would have lived for very long. He was already on the cusp of self-destruction without help from anyone else.

At the centre of this matter there are just Tom Keylock and Frank Thorogood. Nobody else had the motive and their antipathy towards Jones was well known. Thorogood, in particular, thought he could best achieve his aims by pulling the carpet from under Jones in various ways but mostly by isolating him by locking him in or out and playing cruel tricks designed to try and send an already weak and now alcoholic individual over the edge. These tricks carry a certain irony when you consider the equally unpleasant ones meted out by a younger Jones on friends and colleagues.

This Could Be The Last Time

Ultimately, of course, we cannot say with complete certainty who did what because most of the evidence is hearsay but there are enough clues in the narrative to make it appear that it was more than accidental death. Strangely, as I found myself writing about it, I had to stop myself referring to it automatically as a crime scene although it may well have been. There is another twist here which may well have had something to do with the outcome. Tom Keylock had a brother, Frank, in the police force and he was undoubtedly in touch with him over this matter. Whether Frank Keylock was able to exercise any influence on the investigating team is hard to say, to keep the scent away from brother Tom. But it remains a distinct possibility. Frank was a senior CID officer at the time and there was no doubt he had the means. If we pursue this argument and presume, just for a moment, that it did occur, it would also explain, given Tom's closeness to Thorogood, why the latter was not more fully investigated.

In any Sherlock Holmes story, the number of people under suspicion for the crime tends to be limited and so it was with the real-life case of Brian Jones, despite a number of complexities. There are just so many twists and turns. It may be that Frank Thorogood considered that Brian Jones owed him money, although quite why, given the lack of any acceptable progress, is a different issue. If he did, and one source quotes £8k, a very considerable sum in 1969, that together with his natural antipathy towards Jones and the likelihood that the contract was coming to an end would have been motive enough for him to take action. In addition, what happened to Joan Fitzsimons later on is surely proof enough of what he was capable of.

But there was a curious coda. More than 24 years later in November 1993, Tom Keylock visited his dying friend Thorogood in North Middlesex Hospital in Edmonton. The latter, according to Rawlings and Spendel (13, 2016), had suffered from a number of health issues in recent years relating to his heart, kidneys and lungs. He was in a bad way and apparently told Keylock that he wanted to clear his mind of a number of things. Thinking this was to be about provision for the future, Keylock was surprised when Thorogood's tone darkened and he told of something he wanted to say but that he wanted a promise that it would not be repeated while he was alive. Keylock agreed. Thorogood allegedly then said:

Semi-Detached Suburban Mr Jones

> "It was me that did for Brian." … [Keylock reported] "I was gutted and surprised but looking back on it I understood it … The next night his daughter Jan called me to say that Frank had died in his sleep." (133, 2016)

However, as there were no witnesses, it could have been an easy way for Keylock to shift any blame away from himself. For that reason the finger seems to point more and more at Thorogood, who seemed to gain some kind of sadistic pleasure from his actions. Yet while this was confirmed by almost everyone who knew him, the one lone voice eventually disputing it was Tom Keylock. In a December 1993 interview he said:

> "I will challenge anyone on television … to show me evidence of *anything* … Everyone he [Jones] employed he trusted. They kept their mouths shut. Brian used to make them feel at home … You'd never hear any talk about him. He got along with them famously." (108, 1994)

Keylock made this extraordinary announcement a few weeks after Thorogood's death at a distance in time when such things would have been difficult to prove. It was almost certainly untrue because Mary Hallett and The Stones remember it very differently, as did Brian's other contacts at this time, and Keylock, of course, had very close connections with Thorogood.

Whatever his motive, it worked and the searchlight has been concentrated on the now deceased Thorogood ever since. It is alleged that Keylock went to some trouble to destroy certain items at Cotchford although we do not know what: presumably anything that might lead the police to a different conclusion.

Scott Jones (no relation) in the *Daily Mail* had this to say:

> PC Albert Evans was the first officer on the scene, arriving at 12.10am on July 3 as ambulance crews tried to resuscitate Jones. He searched the house and took possession of a number of bottles of spirit and various pills.

This Could Be The Last Time

Now in his late 60s, Evans said his early impression was that there were more people around than the three witnesses represented in the police file. So what did he think had happened? 'Some sort of altercation – drug-induced, alcohol-induced. It was Frank Thorogood who was mentioned – he was the one who had been in the pool with Brian Jones.

'There was nothing at the time to connect Thorogood with anymore. Just feelings … I shared these views with Bob Marshall (the investigating officer). I think he said exactly the same to me.'

In a private letter to the Sussex Chief Constable in 1994, written by Evans after he was contacted by a journalist, he stated: 'I personally was not convinced that we were given the correct story, as put forward by Thorogood.' (2008)

Janet Lawson was a friend of Joan's and when interviewed by Scott Jones in 2008, she agreed with this.

'I went into the house to look for Brian's inhaler. Frank jumped back in the pool, did something to Brian and by the time I came back, Brian was lying peacefully on the bottom of the pool with not a ripple on the water.

'I think because of the state that Frank was in, something had to have happened. I mean, why would Frank have been standing in the kitchen absolutely terrified if something hadn't happened?'

Jan believed that Thorogood had not intended to kill Jones but the guitarist's death was probably the result of horseplay that had got out of hand. (2008)

Yet this final sentence strikes as bland. Thorogood, by that time well oiled with alcohol, may have felt every good reason to despatch Brian Jones to the afterlife. Horseplay or not, Janet Lawson was sufficiently frightened by what happened to her friend Joan, three weeks later, to hide away in her brother's house on an RAF base for some weeks so that Thorogood could not get at her as he had done to Joan Fitzsimons. It seemed the builder's net of influence spread far and wide.

127

What Probably Happened

Early on 2nd July, Frank Thorogood was driven by Joan Fitzsimons to the home of David Bailey in Regents Park with the prospect of doing some renovations. Given Thorogood's erstwhile reputation, it beggars belief that he should have been taken on for more work at Cotchford so willingly, especially by someone so well known.

According to Rawlings and Spendel:

> After his meeting was over, Frank and Jackie [Joan] drove over to see Fred Trowbridge at his Maddox Street office to pick up wages for himself and the workmen at Cotchford. In the 1960s ... everyone in the building trade was paid on a Thursday. This practice was eventually stopped [in the 1970s] when it was noted that a significant number of people would not show up for work on a Friday. (135, 2016)

This echoes the current rather unsatisfactory practice of Working From Home.

But when they arrived, Frank was enraged to discover that Brian had given instructions for all payments to cease immediately, presumably on the entirely justifiable premise that little or no work was being done. So the pair immediately drove back to Cotchford with the intention of having it out with Brian. One can imagine Thorogood's mood. When they arrived Brian was in the middle of an argument with Suki Potier who was trying, in vain, to win him back. Meanwhile, the Walker Brothers' drummer, Gary Leeds, had arrived with a view to practising for Brian's proposed new group. Eventually, after a violent argument, Suki was persuaded to leave and Leeds made some lame excuse to go, there being no prospect of any worthwhile rehearsals being done. So when Frank Thorogood entered this already volatile situation, Brian, at last finding some strength of character, apparently told Thorogood that he and his builders together with Janet Lawson should leave.

> Frank contested that he was owed a considerable amount of money by Jones, almost £8000, and wouldn't be leaving until he was paid. (135, 2016)

This Could Be The Last Time

According to Rawlings and Spendel, Brian had already paid out the then huge sum of £18,000 for building work, equivalent to around £300,000 today. For Brian to still owe £8,000 was ridiculous because, as we know, Cotchford still looked like a building site with many aspects of the work left unfinished. The residual photographs back this up, showing Cotchford as if it were a builder's yard and very messy. However, the situation was temporarily defused by Brian agreeing to settle up before the builders left.

It should also be remembered that Thorogood regarded Jones with total contempt, a middle-class ponce who in no way deserved the huge amount of money that had suddenly come his way through the success of The Rolling Stones. His lifestyle was hugely envied by the East End hard man and the recent period where they could do what they liked in comfortable surroundings was clearly coming to an end which enraged him even more. It is possible that he had been informed that he and his men should leave the next day. On receipt of this news, Frank and Joan retired to the local pub where a considerable amount of alcohol was purchased. From the above we can now understand how the stage became set for the tragic final act and why Thorogood, a very dangerous man when riled, could have been planning his revenge. We will never know exactly what was in his mind, but his thinking must have been affected by the drink he had consumed that evening.

As we know, Brian Jones was at this time a confirmed alcoholic and while in his more rational moments, he saw the necessity of exiting Frank and his men, he was also aware that he was dealing with a dangerous individual. As a result, he weakened his case and tried to pacify the builder into thinking that it was a necessity that was out of his hands brought about by pressure from the London office. To some extent this was true, but Thorogood was not prepared to accept this and kept renewing the argument. Jones was there and obviously an easy target. Subsequently Brian, in a desperate effort to bring closure to what had been a fraught and trying day, suggested a swimming session but by this time all parties had consumed a considerable amount of alcohol.

It seems likely that, while nothing on that fateful day was ever planned, Thorogood was by this time consumed with a nagging rage and, knowing Brian as he did, simply did not believe that he would receive the outstanding

129

Semi-Detached Suburban Mr Jones

£8,000 before he left the next day. Janet Lawson and Anna Wohlin were witnesses to the early part of this arrangement and saw Brian being helped unsteadily onto the diving board. At this point the telephone rang and Janet went back to the house to answer it. Since it was for Anna, she called for her so that both women ended up in the house, leaving Frank and Brian in the pool where they swam about for a while.

One possible explanation is that Frank, on seeing his chance, and having had more than enough of Brian Jones, and there being no witnesses, was easily able to hold him under the water for just too long until he went limp and died. The problem is that this version conflicts with Fitzgerald's account about seeing three men holding Jones underwater. This would mean that Thorogood had been accompanied by perhaps two of the other builders and that all three had been complicit in a murder. But where did these men come from, where did they go afterwards and why were they necessary? Somehow, this seems too blatant, too likely to have aroused the suspicion of the police to breaking point and I prefer to believe that what happened did so quietly between the two main protagonists despite Fitzgerald's detailed account.

According to Janet Lawson, Thorogood, coming to terms with what he had done, swiftly retired to the house, claiming he was looking for a towel, leaving Janet and Anna asking what had become of Jones. Lawson went to check and found Brian still and lifeless at the bottom of the pool. Screaming for help from Anna and Thorogood, both women jumped in the pool to retrieve the now lifeless Brian but not before Thorogood had made a call to get hold of his mate, Tom Keylock, who then high-tailed it back to Cotchford having received an urgent midnight call from his wife while at Olympic Studios, to where he had been asked to deliver Keith Richards' guitar. This was when the band were first advised of the tragedy, except for Bill Wyman who had apparently already left.

Keylock headed back to Cotchford Farm, there being relatively little traffic at that time in the morning. However, according to Rawlings and Spendel, he did not arrive until 3.30 a.m. As soon as he arrived he set about going through the grounds to appraise himself of the situation and who was still on the premises. It was at this point that elements of the cover-up were probably put in place.

This Could Be The Last Time

Apparently,

> … he spotted two men hiding amongst the hedgerows. He made a grab for the nearest and forcibly shoved him back out into the lane and watched while the other scampered away. (137, 2016)

These men were presumably Fitzgerald and Cadbury whose account appears earlier. The problem is the timing. According to Giuliano this occurred sometime around 11.15 p.m. the previous evening rather than 3.30 a.m. on 3rd July.

> 11.25pm: 'A burly man wearing glasses with a cockney accent' appears and threatens the two men, who run back to their car and quickly drive away. (221, 1994)

If this were true and the 'burly man' described was Keylock, he could not possibly have been both at Cotchford and at Olympic Studios in London. Furthermore, Keylock was not 'burly'; rather slender in fact. It could of course have been one of the other builders or a misdescription dictated by circumstances and the night. Yet Fitzgerald claims to have seen the same man at the Hyde Park concert, therefore identifying him as Keylock. So this discrepancy causes a major problem in what Fitzgerald and Cadbury claim to have seen. After all, they apparently never actually signed up to it in a witness statement. If it can be proved that Keylock was at Olympic Studios around midnight, so perhaps the man that Fitzgerald and Cadbury encountered was one of Thorogood's builders ensuring that there were no witnesses to what had occurred. Certainly Fitzgerald and Cadbury had not hung around for four hours after being threatened and whatever happened to Jones did not occur anything like as late as 3.30 a.m. on 3rd July. There then arises the second discrepancy between Janet Lawson's account of Brian Jones being left alone by the pool with Thorogood and Fitzgerald's account of three men holding Brian underwater. Being diminutive, there would have been no need for three men to be involved and the muscular Thorogood could easily have managed to drown him without assistance from anyone else. So apart from agreeing that Fitzgerald and Cadbury did actually attend Cotchford Farm, their account seems somewhat dubious. As Rawlings and Spendel claim:

131

Semi-Detached Suburban Mr Jones

> However, Fitzgerald and Cadbury's failure to intervene and help out their friend, who was obviously in great distress, coupled with Fitzgerald's constant refusal to sign a police statement to this fact [!], leaves his version of events highly questionable. Keylock, for his part, does confirm that he threw two men off the property and his language had been far more colourful than Fitzgerald had previously reported. (138, 2016)

But we are still left with the problem of the timing and, from all the available evidence, Brian Jones' death occurred late on the 2nd July, not early on 3rd, by which time the police were already on the premises.

Rawlings claims to have viewed Fitzgerald's statement at the coroner's office in Bexhill and there is apparently no mention of Fitzgerald ever having been at the scene, let alone that he witnessed a criminal act. It could be that he became frightened of the consequences but, either way, there are a number of holes in his story as indeed there are as to exactly when Keylock arrived back at the property.

SPOTLIGHT:
HARTFIELD, EAST SUSSEX

Cotchford Farm lies in a lane just a short distance from Hartfield which is a village and civil parish in the Wealden district of East Sussex. It lies about seven miles north-west of Royal Tunbridge Wells and the parish includes other settlements, those of Coleman's Hatch, Hammerwood and Holtye, all bordering the northern edge of Ashdown Forest. It has a population of nearly 3,000. Historically the village has been referred to as both Hertevel and then Hertefield.

There were three public houses in the village which Brian Jones would have known: the Anchor Inn, the Gallipot Inn and the Hay Wagon Inn, the latter being mentioned in the narrative. The church holds a dedication to St Mary the Virgin. Hartfield had a railway station until 1967 when it was shut as part of the Beeching cuts. The railway track has been largely replaced by the Forest Way, part of national Cycle Route 21.

Among its famous residents, Frederic Maugham, 1st Viscount Maugham PC QC and brother of author Somerset, is buried in the churchyard along with his son, author Robin Maugham. Frederic served as Lord Chancellor in the period leading up to World War II.

Charles Nassau Sutton, rector of Withyham, wrote:

> The greater part of the parish of Hartfield still belongs to the Sackville Family, and the present Earl De La Warr is patron of the living. (1902)

Hartfield was then alleged to comprise 17,500 acres. Henry VIII was reported to have used Bolebroke Castle as a hunting lodge, hunting wild boar and deer, not to mention Anne Boleyn. It is reported that he once stayed at Cotchford. Henry's half brother, Earl Robert of Mortain, held the area on behalf of the king.

RELATIONSHIPS

What we know, according to Rawlings and Spendel, is that after Brian's death, Lewis Jones had given instructions to remove as many of Brian's possessions as possible and that the rest should be burned. If this actually occurred, it has a strange echo of A. A. Milne's wife, Dorothy, destroying all of Milne's possessions after his death but it could also have been done in part by Keylock to destroy any possible evidence. Yet, in Brian's case, it goes further. It is as if Lewis Jones wanted to wipe out the awkward period that was Brian's life, to virtually erase him as part of the family. This does not seem too fanciful since reading Lewis Jones' early statements after Brian's death, one gains the same impression. It is both practical and detached just as Brian Jones' own life had often been semi-detached from reality. However, another reason comes to mind. It is that Lewis did not want Brian's belongings to become the grisly souvenirs of his son's life in the hands of others. Yet the feeling persists that Lewis Jones was keen to disown Brian as a family member, not only in life but also in death. His handling of his family including Brian's surviving sister was as cold as the aeronautical parts that he dealt with in his job. There was simply no emotion. Brian's death was a practical problem to be dealt with on a common-sense basis and grief seemed to have very little to do with it. This attitude seems to have cascaded down to the rest of the family who did what they were expected to do amongst the great and the good of Cheltenham but did so totally without any warmth or human kindness. Tom Keylock echoes this thought when he said that:

> Brian's father was one of the strangest blokes I've ever met, which is saying something. (138, 2016)

From anyone else this might have struck a chord, but from Keylock?

As part of the immediate clean-up operation, Thorogood ordered the other builders to remove the unused building material and load it onto a lorry.

Relationships

After all, they were not now going to be paid as requested and the only funds on which they might draw would be from the sale of unused materials. However, Thorogood, still angry at having been thwarted, may well have been responsible for lifting some of Brian's possessions before Keylock or Lewis got hold of them.

Lewis Jones' judgement came into question again when the subject of Brian's coffin was discussed. Naturally, Brian being a star, the expectation was that his final journey should be in a coffin befitting of his status and, once again, Keylock found himself in the position of arranging it. Both he and the undertaker wanted to send Brian off in style and, after due deliberation, an expensive bronze and silver coffin was ordered from the USA. This cost a great deal more than the normal coffin but for the undertakers, this was the most important funeral they had done and it seemed appropriate for Brian's fans worldwide. However, even at this stage Lewis demurred, suggesting that something cheaper would have been more appropriate. Perhaps he had not wanted something so vulgar.

Apparently, Brian Jones was buried very deep, about 10 feet down. This was done allegedly to prevent any kind of exhumation by trophy hunters. He was laid to rest next to his sister, Pamela, who had died of leukaemia. His body was embalmed and his hair bleached white. The coffin was completely airtight. Three days after Brian's death, The Stones gave their legendary Hyde Park concert with Jones' substitute, Mick Taylor, on slide guitar. Included was a reading by Jagger of extracts from the poet Percy Bysshe Shelley's appreciation of John Keats, *Adonis*, in tribute and the inclusion of one of Brian Jones' favourite songs, *I'm Yours and I'm Hers*.

Nicholas Fitzgerald comments about Jagger's poetic appreciation of Jones at Hyde Park:

> It was ridiculous, ludicrous I thought. The least they could have done was bring on someone who could have read these words with conviction. Someone like Richard Burton … Instead there was Mick Jagger wearing a white, bow-bottomed blouse that was almost like a minidress over white pants, and with a gold studded dog collar round his neck, piping away like someone reading a weather forecast …

> Vaguely, I was aware that the sham of a recital was over. Road managers [including Tom Keylock] and other helpers were lifting cardboard boxes and opening them, shaking them. A few white butterflies flew out and a lot of dead ones fell to the floor. The butterflies, which had been intended to fly off in a white cloud to symbolize the soul of Brian Jones ascending, had been kept too long in the heat, and even the survivors flew drowsily into the spectators.
>
> I heard a voice behind me saying something like, "That was a bloody stupid idea, wasn't it?"
>
> The last time I heard that voice it had said, "Get out of here, Fitzgerald, or you'll be next."
>
> Panic stricken, I turned and saw a man in a red cardigan and white trousers. He had his back to me. He was burly. I climbed quickly from the stage and made my way around the edge of the crowd. (249/250, 1985)

Charlie Watts and Bill Wyman were the only Stones to attend Brian's funeral because Mick Jagger, accompanied by Marianne Faithfull, was en route to Australia to begin filming *Ned Kelly* (1970), about the outlaw. He could not apparently break this contract. He need not have bothered as the film was neither very good nor very successful. Yet he continued to seek openings for a film career.

Joan Fitzsimons was the divorced wife of Harry Fitzsimons and a cab driver in Chichester. She was also one-time girlfriend to the married Frank Thorogood. Her witness statement to the police was probably orchestrated by Thorogood. She, at the time, was the only chink in the curtain that seemed to have come down over the case and it put her in a very dangerous position. She felt, maybe correctly, that Thorogood had been involved in some way on that tragic evening. Up until this point, it appears that Keylock and Thorogood had somehow managed to sanitize the crime scene by both exiting certain people from the premises as quickly as possible and allegedly attempting to coach the remainder on a common theme, that of denying that they were aware of anything untoward. That they were successful with Anna Wohlin is not in doubt because having made her fairly bland statement, she was quickly shipped back to her native Sweden, out of harm's way.

But Fitzsimons was a different animal and not so easily intimidated. Yet she paid for this in the most terrible way. It would appear that Joan had eventually dropped Frank in favour of a Jordanian man, Mushasier Yusef Ziyadeh, which, despite the fact that Thorogood was married, really upset the balding builder. Rawlings and Spendel advise that:

> The day before Brian's funeral Frank had travelled to Chichester in search of Joan. Relatives of Joan say when he caught up with a terrified Joan she fled, literally running through traffic and the town's back streets until she reached the safety of [her friends] the Laidlaws. Once there, she barricaded herself in as a raging Frank battered on the door. Joan called her relatives who came and escorted Frank away. (180, 2016)

The point here is that Thorogood was doubly upset with Joan, one for leaving him in favour of the much younger Jordanian and because of what she might say now that she was out of his clutches. As we know, she was a cab driver for her family firm in Chichester and had had an ongoing affair with Frank Thorogood. In 1969, she was just 29 years old when, as Aisha Nozari tells us, some three weeks after Brian's death she was found unconscious in the back of her cab. She had a fractured skull and had lost three front teeth. This left her in a coma and blinded for life.

Confirmation of this came from the National Archives (ref. 5145/690) with the proviso it should not be released until 2014. It emerged that, according to her brother, John Russell, she had been very frightened of Frank, just as Brian had been, and she had wanted to talk about how Brian Jones met his end. She even wanted to talk to the press about it. There was no obvious connection between this attack and Thorogood and indeed someone else took the rap for it. The attack was alleged to have been carried out by her boyfriend, Ziyadeh, and apparently he went to prison for it. Yet, that makes no sense as it stands. Why would he have done this? Matters become clearer when we learn that Frank Thorogood had allegedly turned up at Joan's mother's house some hours before the attack, demanding to know

Semi-Detached Suburban Mr Jones

where her daughter was. The relationship had obviously gone very sour. If Ziyadeh had carried out this assault, could he have been paid to do so by Thorogood in order to keep him out of the picture? Such a vicious attack so very soon after the original tragedy. It just had to be something to do with the builder whose web seemed to be stretching ever wider.

Joan's friend, Janet Lawson, went to visit her after the assault and was horrified beyond words to find her friend with a smashed face, her head in a brace and blinded, according to Rawlings and Spendel. Janet was so horrified that she had to leave the room to compose herself and then re-enter. It was a truly evil situation and may have encouraged Janet to change her story later on. This strikes me as the most reprehensible event in the entire narrative.

Initially, it seems Joan had fallen in with Thorogood's requests to help chivvy people off the premises before the police arrived. This would have made a consistent story from those who remained all that easier to establish but something seems to have troubled her later, so that when considering the finality of what had occurred, she must have felt the need to revisit it and tell exactly what she knew rather than what she was instructed to say. You may remember that Tom Keylock once swiftly upbraided Jones for hitting a woman, Anita Pallenberg. Yet when it came to what happened to Joan which was many times more vicious, he does not seem to have raised an eyebrow. A curious reversal of opinion unless he too was ultimately concerned for his safety at the hands of an East End hard man with, apparently, absolutely no scruples whatsoever.

Janet Lawson gave birth to Tom Keylock's child in 1970, calling her Elly. According to Rawlings and Spendel:

> Not long after the birth Janet met and married a man called Peter, but the couple divorced in the mid '80s. Together they had two sons –
> one of whom tragically took his own life in the early '90s. (17, 2016)

Unlike the desperately unfortunate Joan, Janet apparently never lost touch with Tom before eventually succumbing to cancer in 2008, when she died in a hospice. So both of the mistresses of Thorogood and Keylock had very unfortunate afterlives. It was almost as if those who came in close

138

Relationships

contact with Jones, like Fitzgerald, Fitzsimons and Lawson, were thereafter somehow blighted.

But, just as Keylock had doubts about Brian's father, it seems there are many questions about his role in the last weeks of Brian's life. Being a schoolfriend of Thorogood is one thing but Keylock must have been aware from the very outset that his competence had been called into question several times before he ever arrived at Cotchford Farm. And, having arrived there, why did Keylock allow Thorogood to take over so completely and wreck Brian's life? It could have been weakness on Keylock's part but there is absolutely no excuse for the ghastly cruelty he inflicted on the by then alcoholic Jones in various ways and creating at Cotchford a monstrous playground for Thorogood's men and their mistresses. So for Keylock, at the end, to become holier than thou about Brian's father and Jones' effects smacks of being disingenuous, especially when his role on the night Brian died is decidedly doubtful. It rather looks as if Keylock's attitude swung with the wind but what is not in doubt is the fact that he should never have employed Thorogood, given his reputation. As such, Keylock can never reasonably escape a charge of gross irresponsibility and of being at least indirectly responsible for what happened on the night of 2nd July 1969. My feeling is that there was essential information missing from the narrative which, after all these years, will probably never be recaptured.

SPOTLIGHT:
DR C. M. MILROY'S REPORT

Dr Milroy was a Senior Lecturer in Forensic Pathology as well as being Consultant Pathologist to the Home Office. In his Report on the Death of Brian Jones (undated) he writes:

> The first question to arise from the post mortem examination is how Jones died. In my opinion there is clear evidence that Jones drowned. In view of the fact that drowning was the cause of death, the question arises why Jones drowned when he was said to be a competent swimmer. The question was raised as to whether Jones had suffered an asthma attack. It was pointed out by Dr Sachs at the inquest that in asthma, the lungs are light and bulky, indented by the ribs with thick mucus in the airways. These features were not present in this case and therefore there is no evidence of Jones suffering an asthma attack and drowning as a consequence.

> The verdict at the inquest was that death was as the result of misadventure. Jones drowning whilst under the influence of alcohol and drugs.

> The circulating blood alcohol level is equivalent to consumption of around 4–5 pints of beer. However, this is difficult to be accurate about. In view of the fact that Jones was a regular and heavy drinker, the circulating levels may have been produced by a higher consumption.

> Deaths from amphetamine abuse are rare. High levels can be tolerated in habituated users.

This has been quoted in full and readers are invited to make up their own minds as to whether there may have been other reasons for Jones' death.

GET OFF OF MY CLOUD

You will remember from the beginning of this sorry tale that one of the things that Brian Jones craved most was approval by his parents and yet it was never forthcoming during his life. From the very start, his rather curious childhood and the premature death of his sister, Pamela, left him somewhat isolated compared with most young children. It was as if he was the cuckoo in the nest where his parents, Lewis and Louisa, gave all their love, and eventually grief, to their two daughters and appeared to leave him out of the equation. We can put a certain amount down to a stiff middle-class upbringing but even considering this, it seems out of balance.

The resulting isolation had a lifelong effect on Brian and the lack of empathy with others seemed to trickle into all his subsequent relationships, even with those five unlucky girls who bore him illegitimate children. He seemed profoundly unable to offer any of them the kind of love they craved for even a very short period and, as they all eventually found out, in due course he simply moved on. With him it was just physical and of the moment. His relationship with his fellow band members was flaky at the best of times and, as a result, he did not show the kind of leadership needed to hold the group together and progress. He was too busy looking after his own interests. Far from showing any generosity of spirit, he even sunk, on occasions, to stealing from his colleagues. Yet it did not seem to provide any real happiness for him.

His girlfriends, and there were many, could be picked up or dropped at will and when any of them tried to get too close, the shutters would come down and he would never repay the kindness and the consideration he so often received. The most obvious case is that of Linda Lawrence and her parents who went as far as taking him into their home and even changing the name of it to reflect the success of The Stones. The wonder is that once they knew a little of his history, they ever considered it in the first place. It puts him, perhaps, somewhere on the scale of autism in his lack of empathy. He climbed on the backs of other people. There is one notable exception in all

Semi-Detached Suburban Mr Jones

of this and that is Anita Pallenberg who seems to have exercised a strange and rather baleful influence on him, including encouraging him to dress experimentally in certain feminine clothes purchased in the ladies' section of department stores. Yet this can hardly be considered beneficial. But after many arguments and several examples of physical violence and abuse, she too left him. Yet Brian never got over her and right to the end of his short life he pined for her so that even the Swedish stand in, Anna Wohlin, never had much of his attention just as Suki Potier, who seems to have really loved him, also eventually lost out.

When Brian started getting into music in a serious way, he began to use people, like the ever faithful Dick Hattrell, in a disgracefully bad way. He would take whatever he could get from them, especially if they were weak or even just polite and considerate. He simply took advantage, even lifting money from them if he saw the opportunity. He was as totally unscrupulous as he was musically and academically gifted. He stood out from the crowd because he could be charismatic, so people wanted to be with him. But, if they got too close, as in the case of Pat Andrews, they usually had reason to regret it. He left his mark on people in other ways too, like the cruel practical jokes he inflicted on the unwary. These, of course, came back to haunt him when he ran across the unpleasant Frank Thorogood who used such methods, not for humour, but in an attempt to wear him down because he regarded Jones as a contemptible ponce who hadn't deserved his success or his money. But, of course, unknown to Thorogood who was unconsciously playing the class card because he could never be like Jones or have what he had, Brian, by the time he was at Cotchford, was actually in debt. Money, mainly owing to lack of financial skills or even self control, slipped through his fingers as easily as grains of sand and as easily as his failed relationships. He simply refused to consider anyone else unless it meant a leg up for him. In the case of Alexis Korner who proved a better friend than he deserved, Brian was determined to keep him sweet as he knew that Korner held the key to a successful musical career, both early on when he began to display his talent and later when he was alcoholic and down on his luck at Cotchford. Alexis Korner, who perhaps understood Jones best and truly accepted him for what he was, had this to say:

> Brian was into exciting things; clothes, colours, music, being a rock
> star excited him. If they ever dulled down he'd immediately gingered
> them up again so that no one could live with him so they were
> exciting. Brian was a kickster, feeling everything very intensely. He
> always wanted to live at a really intense level, which made him very
> prickly. He would get angry and then suddenly be perfectly all right
> again. (194, 1994)

Some more sceptical folk might simply describe all this as selfish and shallow.

George Harrison, who was also quite close to Brian, regarded him as much like himself in as much as they occupied similar positions in their respective bands.

> When we met, I liked him quite a lot. He was a good fellow, you
> know. I got to know him very well and I felt very close to him
> … Our positions were similar and I often met him in times of
> trouble. There was nothing the matter with him that a little extra
> love wouldn't have cured. I don't think he had enough love and
> understanding. He was very nice, sincere and sensitive.
> (194, 1994)

From the two above examples we can glean that the most satisfactory relationships that Brian enjoyed during his life were with his musical peers. These were the people he got on with best and most respected. Those with whom he had personal relationships outside the music industry would quite justifiably have had different views. His behaviour as we have seen was, on occasions, quite unforgivable.

It was not only his relationships with the other Stones that rendered him eventually unsuitable as leader, despite having formed the group. It was his inability to write suitable songs or indeed complete anything acceptable at all that made him not group leader material, plus the fact that instead of managing the others, he operated a system whereby he looked after himself first, both financially and otherwise. So while he was entirely eaten up with his parents' lifelong lack of approval and consideration, he in turn was never able to show any to others. He became an outcast in Cheltenham because

Semi-Detached Suburban Mr Jones

of his wild behaviour and remained one for the rest of his life despite his ability to pick up and play almost any instrument that was put in front of him. One wonders whether the other Stones were aware of what they were doing in eventually assigning Tom Keylock as minder but, as his name implies, he seemed to hold the key to Brian's final downfall.

Let us consider the attitude of his parents after Brian's death. I was particularly struck by Lewis Jones' statement in 1970. Read casually it may appear that Lewis is coming to terms with his son's death and, in a way, he is. But, read carefully, it looks remarkably as if Lewis is breathing a sigh of relief that, at last, there can be no more nonsense to put up with. It simply doesn't indicate any more love for Brian Jones post mortem than there was during his life.

> We've spent the past year trying to settle down. Brian will always be with us and the fans have been very kind. But the past is past and we don't want to see it revived. All I can say is that I think Brian played his part in shaping the world as it is today. (195, 1994)

There are two things that strike me about this. One is it sounds more like a formal tribute to a political colleague than a son, rather like the inscription on the gravestone, and I think the use of 'we don't want to see it revived' is very telling and a relief. It sounds as if he regards Brian's life as a particularly unpleasant period, for him it may well have been, and it must never happen again. Of course this was the second child that Lewis and Louisa had lost and the difference between the two is striking. Pamela Jones was only a tiny child when she died and her loss was more one of unfulfilled promise, whereas Brian's life must have been a curious hybrid to Lewis. On the one hand, he had not become the dentist or the classical pianist or indeed anything serious that Lewis had envisaged. Yet he was musically gifted; he could play a number of instruments including guitar, harmonica, keyboards, sitar, accordion, Appalachian dulcimer, saxophone, marimba, recorder and autoharp. Yet from Lewis's point of view, he was a failure. The success of The Stones ensured that Brian Jones made a splash. The band may have been disapproved of by Lewis but, to the world at large, it was a triumph, for a while at least.

144

Get Off Of My Cloud

Keeping this in mind, it is possible that Lewis later decided to reconsider his public utterances about Brian's life and tried to acknowledge the more positive side.

> He was extremely sensitive, very deeply hurt. He was naïve to the point that he trusted everybody. He was surrounded by people whom he thought were his own friends for his own sake. When he found out that a lot of them could be disregarded as hangers-on, he was most deeply upset. (195, 1994)

The problem is Brian actively sought out, at least for a time, these 'hangers-on'. He needed applause and approval and, if he wasn't going to get it from his parents, then these were second best.

> One of these silver linings is the enormous affection in which Brian was held, not only in this country, but throughout the world. This was immediately obvious from the one thousand letters we received … and it has been manifested by the fact that Brian's grave has had flowers regularly taken there every week almost without exception since he died. (195, 1994)

And, to verify that, fresh flowers were there as late as April 2024 when I visited.

As we have discussed, Lewis ensured that during Brian's visits home he kept his distance from his own sister, Barbara. That early separation, you might think, would have dissipated when they became adults and outside parental control. But in fact it remained in place throughout Brian's life and when Barbara reported his death to an American friend, as described by Giuliano,

> … the then 24-year-old mailed her several newspaper clippings about his death as if he were some anonymous celebrity and not her own brother. 'Doesn't sound very personal, does it?' sighed her American friend. (195, 1994)

What we might glean from all this is that Brian's family were overall pretty cold and remote and whilst they went through the motions of grieving for first a lost daughter and then a son, it was almost like a pretence. There

Semi-Detached Suburban Mr Jones

seemed to be no heart to it, no emotion. So if we then look back on Brian's life and his treatment of others, particularly where there were personal relationships involved, there is often a coldness and a lack of empathy. The irony of Brian's forever seeking approval from his family is more than matched by his failure to show a similar consideration to others, particularly those unfortunate girls who bore his illegitimate children.

SPOTLIGHT:
GEORGE HARRISON (1943–2001)

George Harrison was a musician and singer/songwriter who came to international fame as part of The Beatles, who might be regarded as the acceptable face of popular music when set against the iconoclastic Rolling Stones. Just as Brian Jones sought to influence The Stones with the introduction of American Blues (such as *Little Red Rooster*, 1964) so Harrison tried to include an element of Indian music and Hinduism into the work of The Beatles.

While Lennon/McCartney were known as the principal songwriters we should not forget Harrison's not inconsiderable contribution with *Here Comes the Sun, While My Guitar Gently Weeps* and other standards of the day. While he was as close as anyone got to Jones and claimed to occupy a similar position in his group, the big difference between them was that Harrison was a very capable songwriter, something that Jones aspired to but never achieved. Jones may have been a superior musician but that, on its own, was simply not enough. Harrison took his starting point from such luminaries as Chuck Berry, Carl Perkins and Chet Atkins so the American influence was also quite strong. Surprisingly, he even cited George Formby.

Unlike Brian Jones, a determined southerner, Harrison was born in Liverpool and was the youngest of four children of Harold Hargreaves (perhaps Hargrove), a ship's steward with the White Star Line. Also, unlike Jones, his childhood was happy due to supportive parents who soon realized that what their son most enjoyed was making music. Harrison met Paul McCartney while they were both students at the Liverpool Institute. Originally part of a skiffle group, Lennon/McCartney formed The Beatles in 1958, rather before Brian Jones had become involved in music in a big way. Harrison became known as 'the quiet Beatle' by accident due to his apparent laconic nature, actually due at the time to a strep throat where he had been advised to limit the use of his voice.

Semi-Detached Suburban Mr Jones

While he was with The Beatles, he felt that his potential would be better served by going solo and during their 1966 tour he was introduced (by David Crosby of *The Byrds*) to Indian music through the work of Ravi Shankar. He spent some time in India, learning to play the sitar but eventually decided his forte was really as a guitarist. We should also mention his Concert for Bangladesh, organized by Shankar. His solo career began in 1968 and lasted perhaps 20 years.

He was also involved in film production through Handmade Films, as an executive producer on such films as *Mona Lisa* (1986) and *Withnail and I* (1987).

He married Pattie Boyd in 1966, a union that lasted just 11 years. After that he married Olivia Arias who bore him a son. It is not generally known that he survived a knife attack by an intruder in his home at Friar Park. He died in 2001 at the age of 58, having been a lifelong cigarette smoker.

AFTERMATH

In the last few days of Brian's life, his mood swings were dramatic. So those who dealt with him were uncertain how they would be received. According to Geoffrey Giuliano:

> On Monday, 30 June, he telephoned his psychiatrist, Dr A L Greenburgh, in the mid-afternoon, urgently requesting a prescription of Durophet … Although reluctant … Greenburgh relented and wrote out a prescription for just ten tablets. How, or even if, Jones ever collected them is not known. (116, 1994)

It is possible that these were the pills that Brian received on 2nd July, as reported earlier.

Against that was some evidence that Jones no longer took hard drugs. So although the hype around Brian's death rested on a drug-fuelled plot, the truth may have been very different. Mary Hallett said that Brian was far too afraid of another drugs bust to get involved again. Most of Brian's contacts at that time agree that he was off drugs, even the notorious Frank Thorogood. Ronni Money declared that:

> We used to have some real long talks and even on the telephone I knew he was really off drugs. The high he was on was the real him. (117, 1994)

And yet the post mortem showed distinct evidence of drugs in Brian's body and there were reports of hash cakes being passed round. Meantime, Thorogood's men were ripping him off on almost every level. Brian was very much aware of this and, at this point, had not received the £100k severance pay from The Stones. He was already in debt and the scene was set for the evening of July 2nd 1969, and the end of Brian's short, fractious life. Brian had apparently summoned up the courage to get rid of 'this bastard' Thorogood and was expecting his severance pay from The Stones' office any day. He was warned not to make Thorogood angry but replied:

Semi-Detached Suburban Mr Jones

> I've got someone on my side that's going to help with any problems. They won't dare fuck with anyone once they see what I've got on them. (118, 1994)

As to who Brian was referring has never been discovered but it gave him enough resolve to deal with the matter. He told all the builders to clear off later on the next evening. This proved to be a big mistake and probably the indirect cause of his death. It is known that he made several very worried calls to Suki Potier, who had by now left the scene, from which it emerged that she thought he was in some kind of bad trouble and she spoke to Nicholas Fitzgerald expressing her concern. This comes out in Fitzgerald's 1985 memoir.

> I'm very worried about him. Something's going on. He's called me three times. He thinks he's in some kind of danger. Says he's being watched. Followed even … Go to Cotchford Farm and see; don't tell him you're coming. Just see if everything's all right. (1985)

Sadly Fitzgerald initially decided against it. He did ring but there was no response. Things might have turned out differently if he had. He seems to have been a weak man. And yet Giuliano's account seems at odds with Terry Rawlings and Paul Spendel who claim that Fitzgerald did visit Cotchford on that fatal evening and was turned away in no uncertain terms by a thuggish man who emerged from the bushes as mentioned previously. We cannot discount Brian's previous paranoia but this time it seems to have been justified.

As we have already discussed:

> Fitzgerald passed on the opportunity to sign his claims on three separate occasions, thus disqualifying himself as a reliable and credible witness. This led the Detective Chief Superintendent that questioned him to conclude in his file that "In my view Fitzgerald was a Walter Mitty type of character". So basically the police humiliatingly viewed Fitzgerald as a total fantasist and saw his claims as nothing more than a publicity gimmick. The book came out with little fanfare and the once young socialite disappeared – only resurfacing when it was reported he had been found dead

Aftermath

in Manchester in 2009 [ironically the same year Keylock died], a wasted and washed up alcoholic. (172, 2016)

Yet another of Brian's contacts who came to an unfortunate end.

I have already commented on the inclusion of substance mentions in Fitzgerald's book and, as an asthmatic, he seems to have gone the same way as his friend, Brian Jones, albeit some 40 years later.

Rawlings and Spendel reveal another surprising twist.

Yorkshire born Lawson is a pivotal character, the key to why Tom Keylock was at Cotchford Farm that night, and the reason he denied it for thirty years. She was a qualified nurse – well spoken and well bred from an upper middle-class background. She moved south to Sussex in 1968 and shared a house with Joan Fitzsimons nearby. By all accounts they made a contrasting pair with Joan divorced and something of a wild child, and Janet reserved and quiet. Janet and Joan struck up a double-date relationship/affair with (the married with children) Tom and Frank who flaunted the situation – often as a foursome – in and around Chichester. (171, 2016)

This illustrates the closeness between the two men.

However, Tom's blatant cavalier attitude to this extra-marital liaison would soon come to its somewhat inevitable climax, Janet found herself pregnant. For the first time, we can reveal the real reason Lawson was at Cotchford Farm the night Brian died, she had gone there to break the news to Tom of his impending fatherhood. (171, 2016)

Janet Lawson gives this account of the events of the evening of 2nd July 1969:

We had wine with the meal and Brian attempted to persuade us to use the outside pool. We all declined, but he swam and we took drinks out to the side of the pool. It was 9.00pm and the floodlighting was on.

He was a good swimmer and was acrobatic in the water.

Semi-Detached Suburban Mr Jones

I think we watched him for about two hours and then I left to return to the flat. (214, 2016)

Two hours seems an unlikely long time for Brian to be in the water in the evening, in July, in England, even after a warm day. Initially the area round the swimming pool would have been lit by only gradually fading daylight and any light from the house but the floodlights were put on later. Although Anna Wohlin came up with much the same story, she adds that, at one time, Brian came up to her to ask for his inhaler, for his asthma. He asked her to join him but she refused, saying it was too cold, a point that further queries how Brian could have been in the water for as much as two hours. We know that Thorogood accompanied a traumatized Anna Wohlin away from Cotchford after the event. Did he use this to coach her as to what to say or indeed what not to say? From a statement she made years later, this seems to have been the case.

It would appear that Brian was very drunk even before he went swimming and was staggering about. Janet Lawson opines:

Eventually Brian flopped into the water and yet despite his condition seemed to be able to cope and made his strokes in the deep end. His movements were sluggish. (129, 1994)

We know that Lawson, being a nurse, helped to remove his body from the deep end of the swimming pool where it was found lying upside down and that she attempted artificial respiration on the side of the pool in vain. But she was, apparently, not there at the time of death.

In considering what was said subsequently we should not discount the varying associations between the people involved. Lawson holds that Thorogood was trying to hold Brian upright on the springboard before he went into the water but we should remember that Brian had wanted Thorogood removed. Did Thorogood use this opportunity to dispose of his erstwhile boss?

According to Thorogood's unreliable witness statement:

Brian was staggering but I was not too concerned because I had seen him in a worse condition and he was able to swim safely. He was a good swimmer but he was an asthmatic and used an inhaler. He had

Aftermath

some difficulty in balancing on the springboard and I helped him but this was not unusual for him. He went in off the board and I went in the shallow end. He was swimming quite normally. Anna was in the pool with us for some of the time, then she went indoors leaving us in the pool. Janet also went indoors.

After we had been in the pool for about twenty minutes or so, I got out and went to the house for a cigarette leaving Brian in the pool … I know I got a cigarette and lit it and I went back to the pool, Anna appeared from the house about the same time. She said to me 'He is lying on the bottom' or something like that. I saw Brian face down in the deep end and on the bottom of the pool. Anna and I got in the water and after a struggle, got him out. His body was limp and we got him on the side, Janet joined us and helped get him out. (03/07/69, 260, 2016)

His Swedish girlfriend Anna Wohlin was convinced he was still alive when he was taken out of the pool, insisting that he still had a pulse. (Sky News – UK, 2021)

Perhaps it was wishful thinking, that she simply desperately wanted him to be still alive but Thorogood's statement does not entirely gel with Janet Lawson's account.

Frank Thorogood – the great rescuer? I think not. There are no easy answers to the precise cause of death of Brian Jones on 2nd July 1969. There are a number of contributory ones like his asthma, his persistent drinking, his volatile behaviour, his previous drug taking, his sacking from The Stones and his dislike of Frank Thorogood. But in the end the most likely cause was the enmity between the two men, although completely unproven and even flatly denied by Keylock after Thorogood's death. There was also the problem that,

… Jones had a heavily enlarged liver and heart when he died. (Sky News – UK, 2021)

This was confirmed in the post mortem notes but so was 'evidence of violence' and 'burns'. What exactly that meant has never been satisfactorily explained.

Brian Jones met his fate in the swimming pool, perhaps being held down once too often by Thorogood, angry that his tenure at Cotchford was coming to an end and with it his opportunities for hounding his employer against whom he seemed to have a burning resentment. If this is true, then Thorogood's witness statement is full of omissions and Tom Keylock, who also initially claimed not to be there on the night but was later found to be, was implicated in a cover-up, fulfilling his role yet again as Mr Fix It. He tried to make out that he was not there at the time, only returning after what might be termed 'a decent interval'. Terry Rawlings and Paul Spendel suggest the following:

> Think about it. It's a perfect way of establishing an alibi! If you were at the scene of the crime, get someone from the scene to ring up your employers asking if they have seen you, knowing these are the very people who when they see you, will send you to the crime scene – unwittingly sending you back to where you had already been. Thus making it appear you had never been there in the first place. (150, 2016)

> This gave him over a two and a half hour window in which to brainstorm alibis for the remaining (or should I say selected) house guests and enlist the help of his brother Frank, who just so happened to be a high ranking CID officer in London. (185, 2016)

We have heard how Keylock himself made what appears to be a statement verified by solicitors on 21st February 1994 confirming his story about Frank Thorogood's dying statement in hospital. Why would he do this? Possibly to divert any suspicion from himself and to apparently bring closure to an ugly incident. Because of his association with Thorogood, a more thorough police investigation might have made much more of the close association between these two men and there is no doubt that if riled, Keylock could be pushed to violence. Incidents on various Stones' tours bear witness to that. Further, because Keylock was in the fortunate position of having a relation in the police force, there was someone to watch out for him. However, there is no evidence that he was directly involved and the likely suspect is still Thorogood, perhaps assisted by one or more of his men.

Aftermath

Looking back over more than 50 years this incident seems like a salutary end to a decade of unlicensed freedom, a warning to the curious. Brian Jones' many incidents combine into a life of unbridled hedonism. He seemed to have totally lacked any concern for others in his fast track to oblivion. Deep down somewhere there was still a trace of the middle-class sensibilities with which he had been born, as in his relationship with Mary Hallett, but he threw it all up for the false gods of rock stardom, adulation, women, drugs and money. Yes, he had talent in abundance but, eventually, the destructive urge was just too strong. He didn't deserve to die like that but it seems unlikely that he would have lived a long life. His health was already suffering. He was effectively the dark side of the original Christopher Robin, what he looked like being at odds with what he became. A would-be Christopher Robin returned to Cotchford to die surrounded by the memories of Milne's creation. Another moment in the remarkable history of Cotchford Farm.

One of the difficulties in this case is the way that the emphasis has subtly shifted over the half century since and this is due in no small part to unreliable narrators, both directly and indirectly involved with the case. In addition there was a network of allegiances, both family and otherwise, that has helped to obfuscate rather than clarify. Rawlings (in an earlier volume) alleges, almost in passing, that Geoffrey Giuliano stole his manuscript and quotes from it liberally but if that were the case why was there no court case to put matters right?

> The memory of a certain American author's liberal (and libellous) lifting of my original manuscript still haunts me to this day. (160, 2016)

On the plus side, Rawlings and Spendel's account, whilst rambling in places, contains the most detailed information and some fascinating photographs of the main participants. As Keith Richards is alleged to have said:

> That cat (Terry Rawlings) has probably got it right. (Back cover, 2016)

But despite the sense of waste associated with the death of Brian Jones, there are three little incidents which I believe sum up both the cruelty and

Semi-Detached Suburban Mr Jones

the sense of waste. Terry Rawlings and Paul Spendel tell us that in the days following Brian's death, Mary Hallett was at home,

> ... and had just settled in for the evening when the doorbell rang, setting her dogs off barking loudly in the hallway. She went out to the glass-panelled door where Frank Thorogood was standing, his finger resting on the doorbell. "He had come back to get his clothes out. I told him that I had police orders to keep the place all shut up and I was told particularly to keep him shut out. He was very angry and called me a fair number of names." Mary breathed a sigh of relief as Thorogood sloped off down the path muttering to himself and disappeared from her life. (113, 2016)

Mary had never heard the Cotchford burglar alarm go off in all the years she had worked there so when it did, a few days later, she despatched her husband Les to investigate. He arrived just ahead of the police, also responding to the alarm.

> There he found stuck between the outer and inner doors at the back of the house, Anna Wohlin curled up in a ball and crying hysterically. (113, 2016)

She too had wanted her clothes and, being thin, had crawled through the cat flap. She could simply have approached Mary Hallett. The police removed her and Mary never saw Frank or Anna again.

But saddest of all, the alarm went off a second time on another day and despite nobody being discovered on the Cotchford premises, the police with Mary carried out a search of the property. They were about to leave when Mary spotted, on the top of the pool where Brian Jones died, a small brown paper package. When the police fished it out and undid it, it was found to contain a set of baby clothes addressed to Brian. A strange memorial indeed and there was no clue as to who had left it there. Since Brian was found at the bottom of the pool and these were floating on the surface, it just seems the saddest refrain; more so than any of the songs. The tide had finally gone out for Brian Jones, never to return.

Allen Klein was an American who at one point managed The Beatles and The Stones simultaneously through his company ABKCO Music and Records

Aftermath

Incorporated. He took on management of The Stones after Oldham, and allegedly carried out a personal investigation into Jones' death. This was allegedly because he had no confidence in the police investigation that was carried out, but Klein died prematurely without a satisfactory result.

It is worth noting that both Jimi Hendrix and Jim Morrison of The Doors also died at the age of 27. Completists might appreciate that Jones played percussion on the Jimi Hendrix song, *All Along the Watchtower* in 1968, saxophone on The Beatles' *You Know my Name (Look up my Number)* in 1967 and provided sound effects and backing vocals for *Yellow Submarine* (1966).

Strangely, Alistair Johns, who bought Cotchford afterwards, refurbished the swimming pool and allegedly sold unwanted tiles from the original at £100 each to fans of The Stones. This, apparently, went a good way towards covering the cost of the refurbishments but it seems to me a rather unfeeling thing to have done. Johns owned the farm for nearly 50 years but had trouble selling it, despite its rich history.

With his five illegitimate children, Brian Jones left an incalculable mess behind him, affecting the lives of a number of families for years to come. One of them, Belinda Marion, who only discovered in 2002 that she was the daughter of Brian Jones, maintains from her own research that the case was not properly investigated and that he was not given sufficient credit for founding The Stones and choosing the members of the band.

> "He formed the Rolling Stones," she said. "He chose every member, he got them their gigs. If it weren't for my father, Mick Jagger would be an accountant somewhere." (Sky News – UK, 2021)

Even now, in 2024, visitors come from across the world to visit his grave in Cheltenham Cemetery, nearly 60 years after his death. Roger Gore, Brian's schoolfriend, tells us that:

> The 43 acre cemetery was laid out in 1863 by my maternal great great-grandfather, George Yiend, mason and quarry master of Gloucester Street. (2019)

Cheltenham seems an appropriate place for the troubled Jones to be laid to rest. Home is where the heart is and in Brian Jones' case it is where he

Semi-Detached Suburban Mr Jones

aspired to be despite his family's rejection. He may have seen Cotchford as a late substitute for this but, alas, it all went horrifically wrong.

I feel that what is omitted from the narrative, due to lack of evidence, is a thorough understanding of the relationship between the more subtle Keylock and the blatant Thorogood and what passed between them during the days leading up to Jones' death. This I believe is the missing link. Pierre Perrone, in *The Independent*, states that:

> With the Stones taking up tax-exile status and residency in France in 1971, Keylock's services were no longer required and he went back to running his own transport company. In the Eighties, he secured another prestigious engagement when he worked for the England football team. He came out of retirement to act as adviser on *Stoned* and was portrayed by David Morrissey in the film. (2009)

These days there are some putative cures for asthma available using mono-clonal antibodies. According to Dr Theodore Dalrymple in *The Oldie*:

> There's a relatively new treatment for severe asthma with monoclonal antibodies – known as biologics – because they are produced and harvested from such living tissue as Chinese hamster ovaries. It offers not merely amelioration or control of symptoms, but virtual elimination of the disease.
>
> A retrospective study of 501 severe asthmatics in Denmark shows that not only can the use of monoclonal antibodies (which have to be injected) prevent exacerbations, which often require hospitalisation; also they permit the abandonment of corticosteroids (prescribed to control severe asthma) and return breathing to normal in 20 per cent of cases.
>
> Great improvement is seen in the majority of other cases …
> Wonderful as they are, corticosteroids have a list of potential side effects to make strong men tremble. (2024)

There are also side effects associated with monoclonal antibodies.

I have compared the lives of three residents of Cotchford from the early 1800s until 1969 and attempted to show how this striking property had

158

Aftermath

played host both as a much-loved home as well as the dumb witness to one of the most reported tragic deaths of the 20th century. Two of our subjects had Cotchford as the background to their formative years but eventually left. The third came to the farm looking for solace that proved ultimately out of reach. But Cotchford Farm is still active, albeit as an Airbnb in the pretty English village of Hartfield. There must surely be more to come.

BACKGROUND

It was a cold blustery week in April 2024 when I decided I would look round the points of interest in Cheltenham where Brian Jones grew up. It seems almost impossible to believe that all this happened 55 years ago. It seems somehow much more recent. The reason for this is that there has been so much publicity about Brian Jones' death, and it still refuses to disappear into the past.

I started where he was laid to rest in Cheltenham Cemetery, an enormous space laid out by an ancestor of Roger Gore, Brian's schoolfriend. This is located not far from the Sainsbury's supermarket in Prestbury and up a side road. There were both outer and inner gates leading into the largely silent world of the dead. Despite the lack of noise, there was still some sense of overcrowding even though its inhabitants had lost their voices and were now forever silent. The atmosphere was suitably sombre.

Even though I had a reference, I couldn't immediately trace Brian's grave and my initial foray through the tufted grass led nowhere. Fortunately, there was a video on my mobile that showed me exactly where to go and, by following this exactly, I then found the grave without much trouble. Beside a path leading to the cemetery buildings, the plot was very much smaller than I expected from photos I had seen and Brian was crowded in on all sides by other unconnected graves. I had been informed that he had been buried next to his sister, Pamela, but for some reason, I could not find this plot. The most poignant aspect was that, even after all this time, there were fresh flowers on Brian's grave and a photograph of him in his prime. It just emphasized the sense of waste. He would only be 82 now. Yet these posthumous gifts after all this time show that Brian Jones is still drawing people in, the only difference being he is no longer in a position to respond.

Cheltenham is exceptionally appealing with its Montpelier shopping centre and plenty of period buildings, a very different background to those of the

Background

other Stones. When Brian was born, the family lived at Rosemead, 17 Eldorado Road, Lansdown where there is a blue plaque (paid for by The Brian Jones Fan Club) and then later they moved to 335, Hatherley Road, also in Cheltenham.

What surprised me was the very modesty of this latter semi-detached property which sits back from the road with a few others in a little inlet. How much it has changed since Brian lived there I don't know but from photographs, it looks plainer and more befitting Lewis Jones' family. However, it's just not as large as I expected or imposing enough. There are what I would describe as more appropriate properties closer to the centre of Cheltenham within the same long winding Hatherley Road, some of which backs on to the railway. The Rosemead property seemed larger and more suitable for the Jones family at the time whereas 335, Hatherley Road seems like a step down.

Brian went initially to Dean Close Preparatory School, Lansdown, before attending Pate's Grammar School, now in Princess Elizabeth Way, Cheltenham, but at the time located in the high street before it was given over to shops. This has an extremely honourable history and goes back 450 years from when its founder, Richard Pate, started it all with a fund bestowed to Corpus Christi College, Oxford in 1574. Its Latin motto is *Patebit tum quod Latuit* or *That which is hidden shall be revealed* which is pretty well the objective of this book. There are currently nearly a hundred staff and, although a grammar school, it has much in common in style with a minor public school. Unfortunately for Brian Jones, while subjects were usually well taught, it gave off a sort of educational stuffiness that was not dissimilar to his treatment at home. Therefore, in true Jones fashion, he eventually felt obliged to rebel against it.

We know that Lewis Jones was the sometime organist for St Mary's Church in Cheltenham. The problem is which one? Strangely, there appear to be three possibilities, all fairly close together. However, it is likely to have been the main Anglican parish church in Clarence Street. It is particularly grand and contains some unusual artefacts. Both Lewis and his wife were musically gifted and so was Brian. Unfortunately he preferred a distinctly non-classical approach, preferring jazz and the blues, much to his parents' annoyance.

Semi-Detached Suburban Mr Jones

Cheltenham is still a gracious town with some fine buildings. Some of the boulevards are pleasantly wide with plenty of green spaces. The Montpelier shopping centre and the Queens Hotel are well worth a visit. Sitting, as it does, on the edge of the Cotswolds, Cheltenham and Pate's Grammar School could have provided an excellent starting point for the young and talented Brian Jones. Such a shame he decided to trash his life. Many young men would have been delighted to have had such a start and benefitted accordingly.

ACKNOWLEDGEMENTS

I would like to thank Lord Strathcarron and Lucy Duckworth and the rest of the team at Unicorn Press for their kindness and support in preparing this book. Their experience and knowledge have been invaluable.

I am also grateful to Geoffrey Giuliano's 1994 book *Paint It Black* which has provided some very useful information. Also, to Terry Rawlings, who, over several volumes, left no Stone unturned in his desire to get at the truth. I am left in awe at his thoroughness.

Also, my sincere thanks must go to my wife, Eithne, who encouraged me to continue despite a severe and debilitating attack of Covid in the winter of 2023.

BIBLIOGRAPHY

Anon, Anita Pallenberg, https://Wikipedia.org/Anita_Pallenberg, Accessed 08/05/2024.

Anon, 'Barrymore pool death – Inquest hears of sexual injuries', *Watford Observer*, 11/09/2002.

Anon, *Slide guitar*, https:/en.wikipedia.org/wiki/Slide guitar. Accessed 02/05/24.

Anon, *Morocco*, https://en.Wikipedia.org/wiki/Morocco Accessed 06/05/24.

Broomfield, N. 'Me and Mr Jones', *The Spectator*, London, 20/05/23.

Cheltenham. en.wikipedia.org/wiki/Cheltenham. Accessed 08/11/23.

Dalrymple, T. 'The Doctor's Surgery – The fickle finger of fate', *The Oldie*, Issue 440, London, 06/2024.

Fitzgerald, N. *Brian Jones: The Inside Story of the Original Rolling Stone*, Penguin, London, 1985.

Giuliano, G. *Paint It Black*, Virgin, London, 1994.

Goodman, D. 'New suspect emerges in possible Brian Jones murder', *Entertainment News*, 15/09/2009.

Gore, R. *50s Adolescence in Cheltenham: A Tribute to Brian Jones*, http://brianjonesblues. co.uk/50s-Adolescence.asp, (2019) Accessed 24/03/2024.

Hayes, A. & Gillespie, T. 'Rolling Stones founder Brian Jones 'murdered', his daughter claims', Sky News – UK, 12/02/2021.

Harrison, G. https: en wikipedia.org/wiki/George Harrison. Accessed 29/02/24.

Hobley, T. The Brian Jones Fan Club, 17/11/2005 Accessed 29/01/2024

Jones, S. 'Has the riddle of Rolling Stone Brian Jones's death been solved at last?', *Mail Online*, 29/11/2008. Accessed 22/02/24.

Jones, S. 'The Rolling Stone's secret son breaks a 45-year silence to tell the astonishing story of how his quest to find his true identity ended in heartbreak – and why he is CERTAIN his rock star father was murdered', https://www.dailymail.co.uk/femail/article-1353783/Being-Brian-Jones, *Mail Online*, 24/07/13. Accessed 03/05/24.

Ko[e]rner, A. *Alexis Korner*, https: en wikipedia.org/wiki/Alexis_Korner, Accessed 29/02/2024.

Milroy, C. M. Report on the Death of Brian Jones, as quoted in Rawlings, T. & Spendel, P. *Brian Jones: Who Killed Christopher Robin? – The Final Truth*, Rock Bookshop, London, 2016.

Nozari, A. 'Rolling Stones star's 'accidental' death called into question by unearthed statement', *Metro*, 16/07/23. Accessed 22/02/24.

Perrone, P. *The Independent*, London, 09/11/2009.

Rawlings T. & Spendel, P. *Brian Jones: Who Killed Christopher Robin – The Final Truth*, Rock Book Shop, London, 2016.

Sutton, C. N. *Historical notes of Withyham*, A. K. Baldwin, Tunbridge Wells, 1902, as republished by Alpha Editions, 2019.

Sweeting, A. *Me and Mr Jones*, The Spectator, London, 20th May 2023.

Wyman, B. & Coleman, R. *Stone Alone: The Story of a Rock and Roll Band*, Viking, London, 1990.

INDEX

Andrews, Patricia, 30–1, 33–4, 34–7, 40
Appleby, John, 31
Attar, Bachir, 66

Baker, Ginger, 48, 94
Barrymore, Michael, 4, 7, 111–12
Beatles, The, 53–4
Berry, Chuck, 35
Broomfield, Nick, 17, 31, 45, 47
Byrds, The, 62

Cadbury, Richard, 117–20
Cantrell, Scott, 100
Carter-Fea, Jim, 96
Cavern Club, The, 51
Cheltenham, 4–5, 11, 20, 25, 160–2
Clarke, Arthur C., 80–1
Colby, Helen (*née* Spittal), 106–7
Corbett, Valerie, 40
Cotchford Farm, Hartfield: current use, 72–3; Jones' death at, 114; Jones' purchase of, 4–5, 73–7; Jones's tenure, 86–91; renovations, 81–3; residents of, 1
Crawdaddy Club, Richmond-on-Thames, 60

Diddley, Bo, 35
Dunbar, John, 97
Dylan, Bob, 62, 63

Ealing Jazz Club, 35, 41
Easton, Eric, 49
Etchingham, Kathy, 46
Evans, PC Albert, 126–7

Faithfull, Marianne, 3, 43, 67, 102, 136
Fitzgerald, Nicholas, 95, 132, 135–6, 150–1; *Brian Jones: The Inside story of the Original Rolling Stone* (1985), 117–20

Fitzsimons, Joan, 83, 105, 106–7, 127, 128, 136–8
Fraser, Robert, 64, 67

Gibbs, Christopher, 79–80
Gibson, David, 120
Giuliano, Geoffrey, *Paint It Black* (1994), 8, 11–12, 17, 25, 26, 29, 30, 35, 37–8, 41, 44, 47, 74, 76, 78, 80, 86, 88, 95, 97, 99, 115–16, 117, 131, 149, 155
Gore, Roger, 13–17, 157
Greenburgh, Dr A. L., 149
Gysin, Brion, 64–5

Hallett, Mary, 75–8, 82, 87, 88, 92, 98, 102–4, 105, 107, 114–15, 149, 156
Hampton, Ralph, 117
Hardy, Françoise, 68
Harris, Richard, 75
Harrison, George, 7, 65, 143, 147–8
Hartfield, East Sussex, 133–4
Hattrell, Dick, 34, 43–4, 45, 53, 75, 116
Hendrix, Jimi, 157
Hitchcock, Alfred, 2
Hobley, Trevor, 120, 121, 123

I Wanna Be Your Man (song), 54

Jacobs, David, 23
Jagger, Mick, 3, 5, 38, 41–5, 49, 50, 55, 85, 102, 135–6, 136; sacks Brian Jones from the Stones, 95–8
Johns, Alistair, 157
Jones, Barbara, 31, 34, 55, 145
Jones, Brian (Lewis Brian Hopkin-Jones): birth and early childhood, 11–12; bronchitis and asthma, 12, 48; schooldays, 12–22; early musical ability, 12–13; interest in trains and trams, 17, 31, 45–6; travels in Scandinavia, 22; casual employment,

165

32–3, 43–4; turned down by architectural college, 32–3; and the Rolling Stones, 41–5; stealing from friends and colleagues, 44; prankster, 46; need for parental approval, 46–7; charisma, 48; health issues, 51; alcohol abuse, 53, 106–7; lack of songwriting skills, 54–6; drug use, 58, 65, 67, 90–1, 106–7, 149; relationship with Anita Pallenberg, 57–8, 62; visits to Morocco, 65; invents The Dream Machine, 66–7; modelling jobs, 68; cross dressing, 68–9, 76; buys Cotchford Farm (1968), 73–7; death at Cotchford Farm, 114; theories of cause of death, 115–32; pathology report, 140; buried in Cheltenham Cemetery, 157–8; illegitimate children, 21, 26, 34–5, 40, 51–2, 60–1, 157

Jones, Kenney, 69

Jones, Lewis, 5, 6, 11, 12–13, 30, 36, 46–7, 55, 61, 134–5, 144–6

Jones, Louisa, 11, 12, 33–4, 55, 61

Jones, Pamela, 11–12, 135

Jones, Paul, 49

Jones, Peter, 99

Jones, Scott, 60–1, 122, 126–7

Juke Box Jury (BBC TV programme), 23

Keylock, Frank, 125

Keylock, Tom, 62–4, 67, 81–4, 86, 102, 104, 105, 115, 119, 120–1, 125–6, 130–1, 134–5, 138–9, 154

Klein, Allen, 156–7

Korner, Alexis, 7, 35, 41, 48, 92–4, 98–9, 109–10, 142–3

Lawrence, Linda, 40, 47, 50, 51–3, 56–7

Lawson, Janet, 64, 113, 115–16, 122–3, 127, 130, 138, 151–2

Leeds, Gary, 128

Lennon, John, 54, 94

LSD, 3

Lubbock, Stuart, 111–12

Marlow Murder Club, The (TV series), 3

Martin, Michael, 76, 78, 84, 91, 102, 104–5, 107

Master Musicians of Joujouka, 66

McCartney, Paul, 54

Milne, A. A., 1, 72–4

Milne, Christopher Robin, 1, 73–4, 75, 87–8

Milne, Daphne, 74, 75, 77, 134

Milroy, Dr C. M., 140

Molloy, Dawn, 40, 60–1, 62

Molloy, John, 60–1

Money, Ronni, 86, 149

Morocco, 64–5, 70–1

Morrison, Jim, 157

Murray, Pete, 23

Nanker Phelge Publishing, 54

Nash, Graham, 94

New Church (band), 110

Nozarti, Aisha, 137

Oldham, Andrew Loog, 49, 53–4, 62

Palastanga, Brian, 38

Pallenberg, Anita, 3, 41, 57–8, 62, 65, 67, 68, 79, 100–1, 106, 142

Performance (film, 1970), 3

Perrone, Pierre, 63, 158

Pilcher, Norman, 4

Potier, Suki, 79–80, 84, 87, 90–1, 108, 117, 128, 150

Profumo, John, 4

Psycho (film, 1960), 2, 7

Ready, Steady, Go (TV programme), 23

Richards, Keith, 20, 38, 41–5, 46, 50–1, 82, 95, 155

Roeg, Nicholas, 3

Rolling Stones, The: Arden tour (1963), 52–3; *Big Hits, High Tide and Green Grass* (album), 67; *Come On* (song), 54; disillusioned with Brian Jones, 84–5, 90; distinct identity, 53–4; fires Brian Jones, 95–7; first LP, 56–7; founded by Brian Jones, 6, 38; growing success, 55–6; Hyde Park concert (June 1969), 135; signs Oldham as manager, 49

Rubinstein, Helen, 67

Sanchez, Tony, 41

Index

Saunders, Jacqui, 8
Savile, Jimmy, 24
Shelley, Percy Bysshe, 135
Simonds, Judith, 48
Six Five Special (TV programme), 23
slide guitar, 28
Spain, Nancy, 23
Stewart, Ian, 49–51
Stones and Brian Jones, The (documentary, 2023), 17, 47
Sutton, Charles Nassau, 133
Sweeting, Adam, 45–6

Taylor, Bernie, 32–3
Taylor, Mick, 95, 97, 135
Taylor, Stewart, 74, 75
Thorogood, Frank, 64, 67, 81–5, 86, 87, 91–4, 98, 102–5, 113, 116–17, 117–23, 125–32, 134–5, 136, 152–3, 156
Top of the Pops (TV programme), 23–4

Watts, Charlie, 38, 95, 96, 136
Whiteley's department store, 43–4
Wohlin, Anna, 105, 106, 116, 130, 136, 152, 153, 156
Woodstock music festival, 38
Wyman, Bill, 16, 26, 38, 51, 60, 136

Young, William, 1, 72, 77

Ziyadeh, Mushasier Yusef, 137–8
ZouZou (French model), 57